The Cash Flow Solution

Tools to Help with Your Organizational Planning Are Available for Sale Online

The Cash Flow Forecaster is a spreadsheet that analyzes the effects over time of monthly income and expense patterns on an organization's cash resources. Given an organization's expected income and expenses for each month, the spreadsheet calculates and graphs net cash flow and the cumulative effects on cash resources (Cash or Debt) over a five-year period. Results are graphed for visualization and presentation.

The Real Estate Calculator is an aid to assessing and making the right real estate strategy for your organization.

The PowerPoint Help Sheet for the Real Estate Calculator contains examples of a variety of real estate assumptions. The assumptions tie to data that has been entered into the Real Estate Calculator. Use this Help Sheet to understand how you can use the Calculator. It contains instructions for navigating the Real Estate Calculator and a sample scenario of an organization considering different financing or lease options for acquiring a property for its operations. The Help Sheet walks you through the process of weighing the options to come up with the right decision.

The two Excel tools and the PowerPoint Help Sheet can be downloaded from the Wiley catalog site for this title. To see more information and to order the *Cash Flow Forecaster* set of tools, please visit www.josseybass.com/go/cashflowsolution.

Thank you,
Richard and Anna Linzer

JB JOSSEY-BASS

The Cash Flow Solution

The Nonprofit Board Member's Guide to Financial Success

Richard and Anna Linzer

Foreword by Philip Horn

John Wiley & Sons, Inc.

Published by Jossey-Bass
A Wiley Imprint
989 Market Street, San Francisco, CA 94103-1741   www.josseybass.com

Jossey-Bass books and products are available through most bookstores. To contact
Jossey-Bass directly call our Customer Care Department within the U.S. at 800-956-7739,
outside the U.S. at 317-572-3986, or fax 317-572-4002.

Jossey-Bass also publishes its books in a variety of electronic formats. Some content that
appears in print may not be available in electronic books.

Library of Congress Cataloging-in-Publication Data

Linzer, Richard.
   The cash flow solution: a nonprofit board member's guide to financial success /
Richard and Anna Linzer; foreword by Philip Horn.—1st ed.
       p.   cm.
   Includes bibliographical references and index.
   ISBN-13: 978-0-7879-7833-4 (pbk.)
   ISBN-10: 0-7879-7833-7 (pbk.)
   1. Cash flow.   2. Nonprofit organizations—Finance.   I. Linzer, Anna.   II. Title.
   HF5681.C28L56   2007
   658.15'244—dc22   2006030499

Printed in the United States of America
FIRST EDITION
PB Printing   10 9 8 7 6 5 4 3 2 1

Contents

Exhibits and Figures

Exhibits

Figures

Foreword

This is a book about innovation and change. New ideas, however radical or wonderful, must be implemented before they can create change. Richard and Anna Linzer match their truly innovative ideas with workable and practical applications that bring about change. Their cash flow concepts have resulted in an impressive history of success for their clients.

This book is important because it addresses so many financial issues that are critical to the well-being of nonprofits. The authors build on their experience and their knowledge to create solution after solution to difficult financial problems. These solutions include understanding how people grasp fiscal information; the benefits that occur when organizations shift to using cash flow for budgeting, forecasting, and monitoring results; how working in the cash flow environment creates the opportunity to use credit successfully as a tool; how collateral can be obtained to access credit; and what cash flow principles suggest when it comes to fundraising, earned revenue, and issues of real estate acquisition and ownership. This is a remarkable set of complex and interlocking issues, yet the Linzers' call on nonprofit board members to rethink their organization's relationship to money is presented in simple and easy prose that everyone can understand.

Richard and Anna Linzer are an interesting set of coauthors. Richard is a master consultant, with formidable experience in the nonprofit field and a track record of fostering innovative programs. Viewed over time, his work is characterized by an insistence on finding better ways to solve complex problems. Anna is an award-winning writer and poet. She brings a clear eye to the material and a strong interest in the precision of words and the progression of ideas. I have known them for many years and greatly benefited from our working relationship.

If every nonprofit organization used the simple method the Linzers propose for reporting on the cash flow position of the organization on a monthly basis, countless hours would be saved each year. Even the most rudimentary change—switching to cash flow reporting—is both simple and powerful. The use of cash flow reporting will make it easier for everyone to understand if there will be a shortfall or a surplus and give them time to react. The ability to accurately predict cash flow is the best, most universal, and most consistent standard for financial management across all nonprofit institutions, regardless of size and mission.

Not everyone will be comfortable with these ideas. Change is often disturbing. Still, we are facing challenges in the nonprofit field that are without precedent. This is the time for new ideas.

The challenges faced by nonprofits are great and are increasing. As the Linzers point out, a lot more people are at the table with not much left over to serve them. The IRS data cited here should be frightening to most nonprofits. The relative scarcity of resources, the added pressures on state and local government, and good old inflation need to be clearly understood. Fortunately, the Linzers present very practical, easily understood, easily implemented steps to help remedy the situation.

All new ideas stimulate resistance. And any bit of innovation will generate an amount of discomfort. The antidote is to get real and do the numbers. The numbers in this book do the job. They offer readers a chance to see just how financially ineffective a cash reserve is in relation to a fully secured line of credit. Or how much money they can really expect from their endowment fund.

Cash flow concepts are a challenge to conventional financial thinking in the nonprofit sector. Yet now is the proper time for us to accept the cash flow challenge that the Linzers offer.

Harrisburg, Pennsylvania   Philip Horn
August 2006   *Executive Director*
                                        Pennsylvania Council on the Arts

Preface

Money matters in the nonprofit sector should be simple to grasp and easy to apply. In most boardrooms, however, fiscal management is neither simple nor easy. This book will radically change that.

Radical was the term our clients used when we started promoting the ideas presented in this book, decades ago. Radical—in the Latin sense of the word, meaning *roots*—is actually an appropriate term to describe our approach to money matters. By focusing on cash flow—the income coming in and the expenses paid out—we are digging down to the elemental roots of successful nonprofit financial management.

Each chapter that emerges from our financial excavation presents a challenge to conventional wisdom. We call into question the usefulness of the budgets we are all accustomed to seeing and we provide a cash flow–based alternative that works much better. Rethinking the essential nature of financial forecasting brings us to a more efficient method, saving time and money. Scrutiny of the monitoring of financial reports suggests a division of labor that makes the process significantly more meaningful to board members.

Our approach to cash flow yields more operational information and offers greater clarity for all board members than they can get from conventional methods. The result is better understanding of financial information and broader participation in decision making.

All board members are able to fulfill their responsibility to ensure the financial health of their organization.

Cash flow concepts provide an analytical basis for developing effective strategies for dealing with shortfalls and windfalls. Our approach provides positive solutions, expanding the choices available to board members. These include the use of fully secured credit to address shortfalls and the substitution of working capital from local sources to reduce or eliminate the need for cash reserves, endowments, and building and equipment ownership.

Cash flow analysis is made simple and easy by two software tools we have developed. The Cash Flow Forecaster's graphic illustrations produce better budgets, more effective forecasts, and instant monitoring. The Real Estate Calculator can save scores of hours spent in boardroom discussions of capital campaigns and real estate strategies. Both Excel Tools are available for sale as a download from the Wiley catalog Web site. Titled the *Cash Flow Forecaster*, they include PowerPoint help for using the Real Estate Calculator. To see more information and to order the set of tools, please visit www.josseybass.com/go/cashflowsolution.

Since we are practitioners who work with nonprofit organizations and board members daily, our prose is lighter than academic writing, the information much more approachable than the accounting literature, and the tools we have developed will make new concepts directly applicable to all board members.

In this expansion of our award-winning book, *It's Simple! Money Matters for the Nonprofit Board Member,* we use the same question-and-answer format—using questions we are often asked—which allows all board members to quickly grasp important concepts.[1]

After decades of working with nonprofit institutions and their boards, we have some definite ideas about what constitutes success in the nonprofit world. Success for the organization is fulfilling its mission in an efficient and effective manner and establishing and sustaining financial stability. For individual board members, success is the ability to fulfill their multiple roles: policymaker, evaluator, advocate, and resource gatherer.

To fully participate in all aspects of the governance of their institution, including the vitally important financial area, board members need to have access to the information that will allow them to solve problems and make decisions. Our work with clients has demonstrated that cash flow thinking and tools can guide board members to success in the nonprofit arena.

The shift to cash flow as a recipe for success is largely a matter of thinking about money in a radically different way. But, as some say, *the devil is in the details*, so here's a look at all those devilish little particulars in the coming chapters.

What's Ahead

In Part I, we explore with you some of the reasons why cash flow concepts are so essential in understanding the sometimes topsy-turvy financial world of nonprofit institutions. Having established a foundation for cash flow thinking, we then look at how a cash flow budget differs from a conventional budget. From there we examine how to monitor and evaluate fiscal information so that everyone on your board completely understands the numbers. Translating those numbers into forecasts helps board members anticipate the future by seeing many quickly developed scenarios.

Budgeting, monitoring, and forecasting set the stage for Part II, a discussion of financial stability—an issue that is on everyone's mind in these turbulent economic times. We recommend borrowing as an effective and efficient way to sustain financial stability. To borrow, you need collateral. Collateral is something that most nonprofit organizations seem to have in short supply, so we focus on developing a new category of volunteers in the nonprofit sector, a group of supporters known as creditholders. We explain how to form a creditholder program to secure collateral needed to borrow. Since we recommend that you borrow from your local bank, we provide guidelines to ensure that your meeting with your banker is successful. Showing how credit can substitute for cash reserves and endowments is next. Once it is revealed how cash flow and credit work in tandem, we examine ownership of real estate and equipment, and we explore earned revenue and discounts.

The finale to this book is a short list of recommendations to board members about the financial policies and practices that we believe grow out of an understanding of cash flow principles.

Using the Book

You may have signed up to be a board member for a whole bunch of reasons—but struggling with murky financial systems or facing rapidly mounting deficits is probably not one of them. You are called upon to interpret financial conditions and to make clear, coherent financial policies. Financial monitoring by the board is inherently tied to decision making. Good governance in the nonprofit world demands that you and every other board member understand the fiscal position of your institution. This responsibility is vital in your policymaking and financial planning, since you are charged with ensuring the long-term financial stability of your organization.

The trustees of a nonprofit organization are asked to look out for the care and feeding of the agency on behalf of the public. You are meant to monitor the financial health of the organization, to take the necessary steps to see that adequate resources are in place to fulfill the mission, and to determine that good practice has been followed in the securing and spending of funds.

This kind of financial planning and decision making requires the analysis of information, the formulation of options, and the initiation of actions that enable the financial resources of the organization to be best used to fulfill its mission. By directing resources to fiscal planning and analysis, board members ensure that financial information will be available to manage the organization. Finally, board members monitor the actions of the organization, so that plans are implemented and resources are used for the purposes intended.

In short, you are responsible and liable for the deeds and misdeeds of the institution. This is such a serious matter that insurance is available to directors and officers and some states allow for limited indemnification of trustees. However, prudence is the virtue that most successfully reduces risk.

To be prudent, you need to be informed. Since fiscal tasks involve all board members, not just those on the Finance Committee, fiscal management needs to be simple and comprehensible. What you want is a financial system that every board member, even the most mathematically challenged, can understand. The benefit of our approach to cash flow is that it offers board members a powerful tool that increases understanding while complementing traditional financial reports. Not only are these new ideas simple to grasp and easy to use, they also enable you to use your own resources to gain access to the operating dollars every organization needs to fulfill its mission.

Indianola, Washington   Richard Linzer
August 2006   Anna Linzer

Acknowledgments

The first bouquets go to our clients, who over the years have taught us everything that appears here. Consulting is always a two-way street. We offer information and we receive information. The issues and the problems faced by our clients have been our laboratory and our touchstone as we have all learned new things.

Ideas often emerge from dialogue. Discussions with James Kolb, Brian Rogers, and Heather Doughty have been especially helpful in shaping the concepts underpinning this book. Philip Horn reviewed the manuscript and offered insightful comments, as did Alan Bicker. Alan also deserves praise for his work on the development of the Real Estate Calculator. His technical expertise and computer literacy will benefit generations of nonprofit personnel as they weigh the relative advantages of different real estate strategies.

Dorothy Hearst and Allison Brunner, our editors, were a joy to work with. Crisp, clear, and always willing to consider a bon mot as well as a bonbon. Books are a team sport. Dorothy and Allison, with able assistance from Jesse Wiley and our fine agent, Elisabeth Weed, brought skills and remarkable energy to the game.

Special thanks are extended to Carl Morgan. A gifted engineer, Carl quarreled with our cash flow concepts just long enough to grasp them, perhaps as only engineers can, and then translated our hypotheses into the first format for the Cash Flow Forecaster. Our heartfelt thanks to Carl.

To Warren Cook, who was brave enough to tackle a vexing accounting question and find the right answer. To family and friends who read, reviewed, discussed, and laughed at our notions, a special round of applause. But none of these good people are responsible for errors and omissions in the text. Those are ours, and we will bear them with as much civility as we can muster, at least under these circumstances.

—*R. L. and A. L.*

The Authors

Richard Linzer provides consultation for businesses, nonprofit organizations, and government agencies. He works with organizations in the areas of financial management, board development, group facilitation, institutional analysis, and strategic planning. Since 1965, Richard Linzer has consulted with more than five hundred businesses, government agencies, and nonprofit institutions in the arts, humanities, education, health care, social services, and environmental fields.

Anna Linzer is a poet and writer and long-distance cold-water swimmer. Her novel, *Ghost Dancing,* was published by Picador of St. Martin's Press and received an American Book Award in 1999. In addition, her poetry and stories have appeared in literary magazines and anthologies, including *Kenyon Review, Carolina Quarterly,* and *Blue Dawn, Red Earth.*

Richard and Anna are coauthors of *It's Simple! Money Matters for Board Members of Nonprofit Organizations; Money Matters! A Kit for Nonprofit Board and Staff Members;* and *It's Easy! Money Matters for Nonprofit Managers. It's Simple!* received the 2000 Terry McAdam Award, Honorable Mention, for outstanding contribution to the advancement of the nonprofit sector from the Alliance for Nonprofit Management.

Richard and Anna Linzer work together as cofacilitators. They have developed a method of facilitation for retreats that uses sequences of exercises in the form of kits and workbooks. The five publications Richard and Anna have designed to be used as organizing structures for retreats and meetings are *The Board Retreat Kit*, *The Board Development Kit*, *The Corporate Retreat Kit*, *The Collaboration Workbook*, and *The Strategic Planning Kit for Public Agencies*.

Richard and Anna Linzer live in Indianola, Washington, on the Port Madison Suquamish Reservation on the shore of Puget Sound. For more on their work, see www.linzerconsulting.com.

The Cash Flow Solution

Part I

Seeking a New Solution
Using Cash Flow

The Case for Cash Flow

U nderstanding how a nonprofit works today, and how it is likely to perform in the coming years, is fundamentally rooted in an understanding of its cash flow. Without an ongoing awareness of how funds enter and leave the institution's coffers, annual budgets or records of past experience, even ones that are laboriously composed, may offer little operational help to board members. It is time for the boards of nonprofit institutions, both large and small, to consider changing their approach to money matters. This means moving away from an almost singular preoccupation with assets and liabilities and toward a greater awareness of cash flow.

For change to take place, incentives or benefits must occur that prompt different actions. In this chapter the case for adding cash flow budgeting, forecasting, and monitoring to the board's arsenal of fiscal tools is bolstered by a set of powerful incentives and significant benefits.

What are the incentives and the benefits of using cash flow?

The clarity of cash flow budgets is what makes them so valuable to board members. Since these documents combine actual income and expense within the fiscal cycle of the institution, they provide more operational information. Board members gain a better understanding of the financial position of their organization and can thus participate more fully in problem solving and decision making. Greater participation is the key to ensuring that all board members can perform their fiduciary duties on behalf of the institution.

Cash flow forecasts provide a practical basis for projecting income and expense into the future. By capturing the dynamic quality of an institution's annual or multiple-year financial cycle, these forecasts provide the opportunity to anticipate and prepare for future events. Cash flow monitoring establishes an ongoing awareness of fiscal position.

Cash flow analysis leads to an understanding of three key factors in nonprofit financial management:

- Money, whether raised, earned, or borrowed, costs money to secure.

- Inflation is of profound significance in the nonprofit arena and must always be considered.

- Time and timing are critical elements in nonprofit financial management.

Cash flow thinking allows tools to be designed to address financial questions confronting any nonprofit institution. The Cash Flow Forecaster and the Real Estate Calculator are computer software that board and staff members can use to rapidly explore complex problems. The Cash Flow Forecaster provides graphic illustrations that allow board members "to see the money," a clear benefit for those who shy away from numbers in the boardroom. The Real Estate Calculator allows different real estate strategies to be instantly compared and contrasted. Both tools dramatically reduce the time necessary to perform these functions.

A major incentive for using cash flow concepts is that they provide the basis for dealing with financial shortfalls and windfalls. Shortfalls can be addressed through the use of fully secured credit.

Credit used to provide locally obtained working capital reduces or eliminates the need to create cash reserves or endowments. Windfalls should be spent for operations, to pay back debt, or to expand programs and services.

Cash flow principles can be applied to questions of ownership versus leasing of real estate and equipment. In addition, earned revenue strategies can be assessed in terms of their impact on cash flow.

Should we change our current system of accounting?

Most nonprofit institutions have their books set up on the accrual basis of accounting. Accrual-basis accounting recognizes expenses when they are incurred and revenues when they are earned, rather than when cash changes hands. This approach to accounting is standard, valuable, and a boon to the keeping of accounts in the commercial world. Yet, for many nonaccountants or people without financial training, the terminology and reports generated by this system can be quite daunting and in some cases opaque.[2]

The cash flow budgets and reports we describe in this book are simple and easy for everyone to understand. Cash-basis accounting records only those events that involve the exchange of cash and ignores transactions that do not involve cash. The financial picture presented by our approach to cash flow is not as finely detailed as the accrual-basis system, yet for board members the grasp of operations provided by focusing on cash flow more than compensates for its inherent simplicity.

Lest any certified public accountant (CPA) reading this book feel that we are making even the slightest criticism of that valuable profession, please allow us to note that the German poet Goethe is quoted as describing accounting this way: "Double entry bookkeeping is one of the most beautiful discoveries of the human spirit." Our sentiments exactly![3]

Traditional accounting, with all the bells and whistles that pertain to nonprofit institutions, still has an important role to play in generating periodic financial reports and the audits requested by funding agencies. So hang on to your current system—but supplement it with the approach that we propose and watch the improvement at your next board meeting.

If every board member can understand and apply cash flow concepts, then the burden that normally falls to the finance committee can be relieved. And it must be, since every board member bears financial responsibility for a nonprofit institution. Cash flow concepts allow everyone to participate in the problem solving and decision making that lie at the heart of good governance.

Cash flow budgets, reports, and forecasts using twelve-month recording of income and expense are dynamic in contrast to conventional balance sheets. A balance sheet is a snapshot of a fiscal moment in time. A cash flow budget, report, or forecast is like watching a movie in which income and expense costar with time to express the ebbs and flows of your organization's financial position.

Money and money matters generate a considerable amount of anxiety in most boardrooms. Cash flow budgets, forecasts, and reports provide a great deal of information that directly addresses the operational concerns of the organization. For example, in determining how to deal with shortfalls and with windfalls, cash flow analysis provides the basis for better decisions in the boardroom. Cash flow is reality based; it increases the range of options available to board and staff members confronted by questions such as whether to build a cash reserve or establish a fully secured line of credit with the bank.

Cash flow concepts open the door to a thoughtful assessment of financial policies and practices that may be popular but are also fiscally very inefficient. The creation of endowments, the ownership of buildings and equipment, and even the virtues of earned revenue strategies can all be viewed through a cash flow lens with surprising results.

Finally, because so many board members are successful businesspeople in their nine-to-five lives, the importance of cash flow needs to be emphasized. These board members frequently see the nonprofit sector as just an underdeveloped version of the commercial world, and many translate their notion of good business practices directly into recommendations for financial policies for their nonprofit institution. The cash flow concepts that we use throughout this book place very little emphasis on the accumulation of assets by nonprofit institutions. This is baffling to some business-oriented board members. As we demonstrate, however, it makes perfect sense once you grasp the importance of cash flow to the nonprofit sector.

Why shouldn't a nonprofit be more like a business?

In both the commercial world and the nonprofit sector, cash flow is important, particularly as a tool for understanding operations. Yet, as any businessperson will tell you, the bottom line in the commercial sector is all about assets and liabilities. For nonprofit institutions, cash flow is uniquely important—and here are some of the reasons why.

First, businesses are creatures of the marketplace; nonprofits are creatures of the tax collector. After all, without a charter from the state and feds, tax-exempt organizations could not offer deductions for contributions and avoid most of the taxes businesses pay. Second, the ways in which the two types of organizations are allowed to raise money are not the same. As we shall see, the rules that apply to this money create some profound differences.

Businesses sell equity (ownership) to investors in the form of stocks, bonds, partnerships, and venture arrangements. Once the equity has been sold, businesses have a great deal of flexibility in how and for what they spend their money. The notion that in business "cash is king" is just another way of paraphrasing Yogi Berra's line: "Cash, why it's just as good as money."[4]

Yet in the remarkably regulated financial environment in which nonprofits operate, even cash is not always a liquid asset (*liquid assets* are funds in a form such as a mutual fund or savings account from which they can be easily withdrawn and spent). Restricted cash may be in the bank account but not available for any purpose other than the specific one dictated by the funding authority. This factor alone can create a fiscal crisis for otherwise seemingly solvent nonprofit institutions.

Nonprofits are prohibited from selling equity to anyone. Instead, they are allowed to receive tax-deductible gifts and grants, which often come with strings attached.

Businesses can use their profits (what is left over when all the bills have been paid) to pay for their activities. Nonprofit institutions are often contractually bound to observe government or foundation requirements that any funds left over from grants be refunded rather than switched into different budgetary areas.

Both businesses and nonprofit institutions can borrow money. So the major difference is this: Businesses sell equity and distribute profits to investors and to the government in the form of taxes; nonprofits receive tax-deductible grants and gifts that are meant to be spent for the social purpose for which the organization was formed.

Businesses have a very different annual fiscal cycle from that of their nonprofit counterparts. Businesses mobilize money through the sale of equity, or they use their profits or borrowing to provide the funds they need to operate. At the end of the fiscal year they distribute earnings in the form of dividends and taxes.

The nonprofit organization is continually soliciting gifts and grants, attempting to earn revenue, and occasionally borrowing. But because they have no equity to sell, nonprofit organizations do not engage in distribution to investors and in many cases pay little, if anything, in federal, state, or local taxes. Therefore, the fiscal cycle for a nonprofit organization is only about cash flow: income in and expenses out.

It is the central importance of cash flow in the nonprofit world that prompts us to examine it much more carefully. In the next chapter, we offer you the opportunity to root out for yourself the differences between conventional budgets and cash flow budgets.

2

Annualized Summary Budgets and Cash Flow Budgets

Financial management typically starts with the preparation of a budget. The allocation of income and expense for a given period, usually the coming year, represents a quantification of the organization's plans. The formats used to create budgets in the non-profit sector have traditionally been influenced by the forms created by funding sources. If a federal agency or the XYZ Foundation asks your institution to submit a budget with its application form, it will usually suggest a format that is consistent with its review process. Whether the form of the budget requested is useful to your organization is the subject we are about to debate.

In this chapter we show two different versions of the same budget, one an annual summary budget that is typically used by most nonprofit institutions, and the other the cash flow budget we use with our clients. We also demonstrate a streamlined version of the cash flow budget for those of you who are diet conscious when it comes to financial reports.

How does a cash flow budget compare with the budget we see at every board meeting?

A cash flow budget clarifies and simplifies financial matters. If a picture is worth a thousand words, then the graphic presentation of a budget has to be worth at least a hundred numbers. The budget that most of us have seen since childhood is what we call an annualized summary budget (ASB). We use that name because the ASB budget format presents the total income and expenses for one year in a single column. You have been there before, but Exhibit 2.1 shows it anyway, just to remind you.

Notice that your eye runs rapidly down the column to the bottom line, which in this case is an intentional—though rare—zero. You might be tempted to glance at the income figures to see where the money is coming from, perhaps noting the $225,000 for earned income, or even wondering why grants, donations, and gifts are presented in separate categories. You might think that the salaries in the expense column are not so hot, but those consulting fees are just outrageous. And what about printing? Isn't printing a trifle excessive at 13 percent of the total budget?

Exhibit 2.1. Annualized Summary Budget: Fiscal Year 2004–2005.

Income	
1. Grants	120,000
2. Donations	50,000
3. Gifts	35,000
4. Earned Revenue	225,000
TOTAL INCOME	430,000
Expense	
5. Salaries	244,992
6. Fringe Benefits	53,892
7. Part-Time Wages	15,000
8. Consulting Fees	7,500
9. Rent	22,000
10. Utilities	5,500
11. Legal and Accounting	13,500
12. Supplies	12,616
13. Printing	55,000
TOTAL EXPENSE	430,000
Balance	0

Typically, these questions, and many others, will have to remain unanswered until the next board meeting, when, if you remember, you might ask them. Unless, of course, you are a very shy person, ever hopeful that someone else will have the courage to broach the subject and risk looking like a fool for not completely understanding the institution's budget.

Because it is a convention, you may not notice, at least not consciously, that all the numbers are a summary for the entire year, which leaves you clueless about what is happening on a daily, weekly, monthly, or even quarterly basis.

On the other hand, the cash flow budget, with its accompanying footnotes, reveals a great deal more information. An annual cash flow budget, which starts with the cash in the bank and is divided into monthly segments, integrates money with the time that will be passing as the year progresses.

The cash flow budget shown in Exhibit 2.2 uses the same numbers as the annualized summary budget, but it looks quite different.

In this case, notice that items of income and expense are viewed on a monthly basis. Some items are the same month after month; these are called *fixed income* or *fixed expenses*. Other items increase or decrease on a monthly basis, and these are called *variable* income or expenses. It likely that your organization's budget will contain a mixture of fixed and variable figures for both income and expense. Yet in the conventional budget you may have no sense of which is which, since the summary totals presented do not distinguish between fixed and variable items.

What does the cash flow budget give us that we don't already have in the annual summary budget?

Purely for illustrative purposes we started both budgets with zero dollars in the bank and end the same way. The annual summary budget provides a sense of the projected solvency of the institution

Exhibit 2.2. Sample Cash Flow Budget: Fiscal Year 2004–2005.

	Jan.	Feb.	Mar.	Apr.	May	June
Income						
1. Grants	0	5,000	15,000	20,000	30,000	0
2. Donations	5,000	10,000	5,000	2,000	5,000	2,000
3. Gifts	4,000	4,000	0	7,000	2,000	3,000
4. Earned revenue	21,000	13,000	18,000	16,000	13,000	35,000
TOTAL INCOME	30,000	32,000	38,000	45,000	50,000	40,000
Expense						
5. Salaries	20,416	20,416	20,416	20,416	20,416	20,416
6. Fringe benefits	4,491	4,491	4,491	4,491	4,492	4,492
7. Part-time wages	5,000	8,000	2,000	0	0	0
8. Consulting fee	0	0	0	0	0	0
9. Rent	2,000	2,000	2,000	2,000	2,000	2,000
10. Utilities	500	500	500	500	500	500
11. Legal and accounting	3,500	2,000	2,500	500	500	500
12. Supplies	2,093	1,593	1,093	1,093	592	1,092
13. Printing	3,000	1,000	2,000	3,000	1,500	6,000
TOTAL EXPENSE	41,000	40,000	35,000	32,000	30,000	35,000
RUNNING TOTAL	–11,000	–19,000	–16,000	–3,000	17,000	22,000

July	Aug.	Sept.	Oct.	Nov.	Dec.	Total
0	5,000	15,000	1,000	10,000	10,000	120,000
1,000	3,000	2,000	5,000	4,000	6,000	50,000
4,000	2,000	1,000	3,000	2,000	3,000	35,000
25,000	15,000	2,000	17,000	24,000	26,000	225,000
30,000	25,000	20,000	35,000	40,000	45,000	430,000
20,416	20,416	20,416	20,416	20,416	20,416	244,992
4,492	4,492	4,492	4,492	4,492	4,492	53,900
0	0	0	0	0	0	15,000
0	3,000	4,500	0	0	0	7,500
2,000	2,000	2,000	2,000	2,000	0	22,000
500	500	500	500	500	0	5,500
500	500	1,000	1,000	1,000	0	13,500
1,092	1,092	1,092	1,092	592	92	12,608
11,000	13,000	8,000	5,500	1,000	0	55,000
40,000	45,000	42,000	35,000	30,000	25,000	430,000
12,000	–8,000	–30,000	–30,000	–20,000	0	0

at the end of the year. It does not directly provide much information about the operations and their relationship to time. In contrast, the cash flow budget allows your eye to quickly chart out the ebb and flow of funds during the year. As you move along the running or cumulative total line, you may notice that the first four months of the year and four of the five last months of the year all end with negative numbers. Sweat could be pouring from your brow at these negative figures. Perhaps you are rethinking your tenure on the board. Then, suddenly you are reassured by seeing that this organization earns its money in May, June, and July, and usually finishes strong in December.

Imagine yourself as a new board member, sitting in monthly board meetings during those first four months and wondering if this is a sinking ship. The annual summary budget is not going to be very helpful to you when the institution hits those months of negative numbers. Did anyone tell you that the financial picture in this organization can make a death-defying roller coaster look like a child's toy?

How can this cash flow budget be streamlined further?

Time is increasingly precious, and perhaps nowhere more than in the boardroom. As a board, you and your fellow members are called upon to plan, decide, and direct the financial aspects of an organization—all this without micromanaging the staff who provide the information that establishes the groundwork for each of these functions. You are legally liable for the finances. The staff members, acting as your agents, are obliged to ensure that budgets and reports are accurate.

Understanding and making good use of the organization's financial statements is one of your most important duties as a nonprofit board member. Yet just saying the words *financial management* to many people in the nonprofit sector evokes a wince.

One of the beauties of cash flow thinking is that information can be compressed to ever more basic levels, allowing for a quick review. For example, a cash flow budget can be summarized, taking a minimalist approach to budgeting that can be easily grasped and understood by board members and staff. The summary form shown in Exhibit 2.3 has been pared down to the absolute minimum, so that only monthly dates, income and expense totals, and the running total are presented. People who want more detail can easily reference the annual cash flow budget or the monthly cash flow projections that have been used to create this summary.

This ultra-slim budget can be used to quickly convey information to the reader. In a summary budget, add a note that reflects the beginning balance of cash on hand and ends with the increase or decrease of cash at the end of the year. The summary cash flow budget also provides the basic information necessary to generate charts or graphs to help some readers better understand the dynamic quality of your annual cash flow.

Can graphically displaying this information tell me more?

Sometimes portraying numbers graphically does aid understanding.

Translating a conventional summary budget into graphic form helps a little, but presenting a monthly cash flow budget in graphic form is a definite winner. Figures 2.1 through 2.4 give some examples of the graphics that you can use to get the information across to everyone who you want to see the fruits of your fiscal labors.

As you can see, the picture of income and expense provides a great deal of information in a compact and easily accessible form. For example, in the graph on income and expense it is clear that both income and expense fluctuate in a relatively narrow band, with no big peaks and valleys in either category.

When income and expense are merged, it's easy to see that the institution is running with a major spike in income in May, then a

Exhibit 2.3. Summary Cash Flow Budget: Fiscal Year 2004–2005.

	Jan.	Feb.	Mar.	Apr.	May	June	July	Aug.	Sept.	Oct.	Nov.	Dec.	Total
Income	30	32	38	45	50	40	30	25	20	35	40	45	430
Expense	41	40	35	32	30	35	40	45	42	35	30	25	430
RUNNING TOTAL	–11	–19	–16	–3	17	22	12	–8	–30	–30	–20	0	0
CUMULATIVE TOTAL	–11	–19	–16	–3	17	22	12	–8	–30	–30	–20	0	0

Note: All figures are in thousands. Since the year started at zero, the cumulative total is identical to the running total.

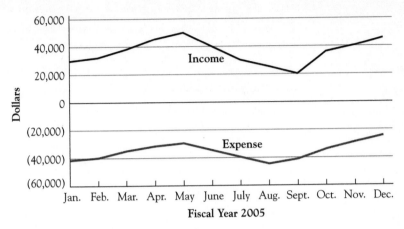

Figure 2.1. Monthly Income and Expense.

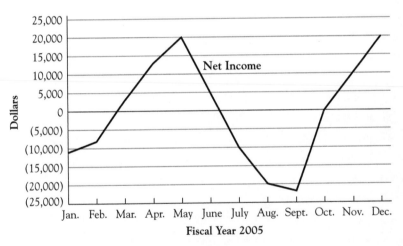

Figure 2.2. Cash Flow (Income and Expense).

slow summer that gradually resolves itself as fall and winter figures begin to reflect the growing income during these seasons. For much of the year, the institution has negative numbers on a monthly basis.

The Cash Flow and Accumulated Cash or Debt graph in Figure 2.3 appears this way, because we intentionally specified no surplus or shortfall at the end of the prior year.

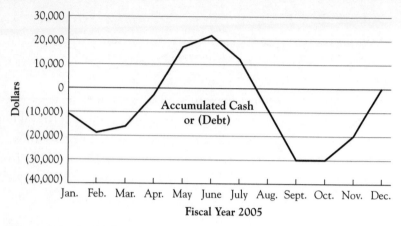

Figure 2.3. Cash Flow and Accumulated Cash or (Debt):
Zero Balance to Start.

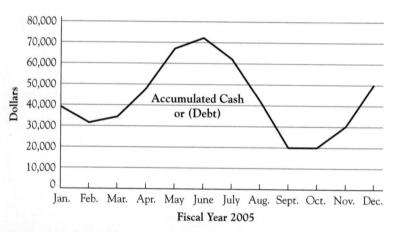

Figure 2.4. Cash Flow and Accumulated Cash or (Debt):
$50,000 Balance to Start.

The graph would look very different with a starting surplus or shortfall. For example, if the organization had started the year with $50,000 in the bank, the graphic image for Accumulated Cash or Debt would look like Figure 2.4.

Notice that the shape of the curve remains the same, but the curve is elevated above the zero line that differentiates positive numbers from negative numbers. As the curve moves up, you can see that no months are spent in a deficit position.

In a cash flow budget you are seeing the money as it moves through the fiscal year. For visual learners, this graphic portrayal is very useful. But what about those of us who cherish words—those wonderful descriptive sentences that convey meaning to us in poetry or prose? In the next chapter we will join our cash flow budget to footnotes that will surely satisfy every learning style and make life easier for a lot of people who experience just a touch of anxiety around numbers.

3

All About Footnotes

The financial reality of the nonprofit sector has been likened to a looking-glass world in which commercial concepts are twisted into unimaginable shapes. The fun house mirror effect of many nonprofit fiscal policies has plenty of reasons, but we will leave it to others to explore this strange and exotic terra incognita. Instead, as practitioners, we will come right out and offer a practical method for cutting through the financial fog. In this chapter we discuss footnotes for every item in our cash flow budget. For those of you who had terrible experiences with tedious footnotes in school, rest assured, our approach will just make the cash flow budget that much more informative.

How can we make the cash flow budget even more useful?

Footnotes to the cash flow budget expand its usefulness. The footnotes accompanying the cash flow budget provide a running commentary. The footnotes give the story behind each and every item of income and expense in the cash flow budget. You should use the line numbers to tie the footnotes to the corresponding items on the budget. (Note: For a given organization, some items may seem to stand on their own without need for further description, but in general it's best to explain everything. When you let something "go without saying," it often just goes and gets lost in the shuffle.) You have the information you need before the meeting, and you still have the option of asking for more.

Here are the footnotes for the cash flow budget presented in Figure 2.2:

1.   *Grants*. The total amount of grants anticipated this year is $120,000. Of this amount, $50,000 has been secured as part of a multiyear grant from the state. Another $40,000 is highly probable, since we are asking for funds from agencies and foundations that have demonstrated a strong interest in our activities or have shown a historical interest in funding our programs. This leaves $30,000 that is speculative. By the end of the first quarter, we will have proposals pending to five new foundations and six corporations.

2.   *Donations*. The first part of this amount is received as part of our annual auction and year-round volunteer telemarketing campaign. Last year the auction raised $15,000. It should do that well or better this year. Consequently, we are forecasting that the auction will raise $20,000 this year.

The telemarketing program has generated a fairly consistent $2,000 to $3,000 per month, with the exception of a sharp dip in midsummer and some higher numbers in October, November, and December. We believe that at least $20,000 can be considered highly probable from this source.

The balance of the $50,000 scheduled for donations is speculative. We believe that the auction and the telemarketing will deliver these funds above and beyond our estimates, but we cannot be certain of achieving this goal. To increase our chances of reaching our mark, we will be using more part-time helpers for the auction this year, and we will be placing emphasis on obtaining more items and greater attendance at the event.

3.   *Gifts*. We differentiate between donations, which are contributions made as a result of direct solicitation through telemarketing or as income from our annual auction, and gifts, which are contributions that come directly from friends or associates of the organization.

Most of our gifts come from planned giving. Although it is difficult for us to estimate the arrival of funds, our experience indicates that roughly $25,000 per year will come from this source. The balance of the $35,000 allocated to this category, while speculative, should come from a program that was initiated last year. We have asked board and staff to secure matching funds for their gifts to the organization, and we are confident that we will obtain $10,000.

4.   *Earned Revenue*. The services we provide give us this constant source of cash.

5.   *Salaries*. The amounts provided for members of the staff break down by position as follows:

- Executive Director: $40,000
- Assistant Director: $35,000
- Clinical Supervisor: $25,000
- Development Director: $20,000
- Two Clerical Staff at $16,500 each: $33,000
- Four Field Workers at $23,000 each: $92,000
- TOTAL SALARIES: $245,000

6.   *Fringe Benefits*. We calculate fringe benefits at 22 percent of base salary. They include our health plan through Group Health, the pension plan we offer through Metropolitan Life, and the portion of Social Security paid by the organization ($245,000 × .22 = $53,900). Divided by 12, this amount equals $4,491.66 per month.

7.   *Part-Time Wages*. This amount is projected for assistance with our annual auction. This year, it is estimated that we will require up to 2,500 hours of effort. Based on an average cost of $6 per hour for this help, we have budgeted $15,000 to be spent between January and March (2,500 × $6 = $15,000).

8.   *Consulting Fees*. Our strategic plan is being developed by a planning and consulting firm that will work for a total of 50 hours on this project (50 hours × $150 per hour = $7,500).

9. *Rent.* We expect to pay rent in 11 months this year. In December we will be moving into a rent-free space that has been made available to us by a local real estate developer who has room in one of his buildings. We can use the space for two years. At the end of this period, we will be asked to pay market-value rent.

10. *Utilities.* We have also budgeted utilities on an 11-month basis. The new space will be provided to us without utility charges for the first year.

11. *Legal and Accounting.* These services are higher than usual this year. We will be audited for the first time and will incur higher fees during the first three months of the year. Our normal legal retainer is $500 per month, and this year an additional $500 has been included for accounting services during the months of September, October, and November. No payments are scheduled for December.

12. *Supplies.* This has always been an important expense category for us. The supplies are vital to the service we perform. With the exception of January, which is usually a costly month, our normal monthly cost is $1,093. During May, November, and December, our inventory of supplies is always allowed to decline.

13. *Printing.* Printing continues to be a major expense item because our publications are in considerable demand. Printing schedules are timed to coincide with our major program activities.

How do footnotes apply to every board member?

Financial reporting in the nonprofit sector is not as standardized as you might think. Exotic and creative terms, as well as interesting and sometimes arcane concepts, seep into even the most conventional fiscal documents. Since you may have better things to do with your life than learning a new financial language, it makes sense to use footnotes to spell out exactly what the numbers mean and the logic that informs them. This lends considerable clarity to budgets, and it also helps to illuminate shaky assumptions that may need to be challenged before things get out of hand.

For a board member, the benefit of reviewing these footnotes is that they tell the story behind each number. In a matter of moments you can have your questions answered about the various assumptions and details that the numbers reflect. Given a cash flow budget—with accompanying footnotes—in advance of the board meeting, you can quickly and easily prepare yourself for the fruitful financial discussions that will occur.

From the perspective of staff members, preparing the footnotes for the cash flow budget provides an opportunity to amplify the meaning of individual items in the budget. The formulas and assumptions used to develop specific income or expense projections can be illustrated through the footnotes. Your institution's game plan can be illuminated both in prose and in the numerical items presented as part of the cash flow budget. If you have ever faced tough financial questions during a board meeting, you can appreciate the value of "prefiguring" what is being conveyed by your cash flow budget.

Better information, in terms of both the operations of your institution and the greater clarity afforded by footnotes, can enhance the experience of every board member. And that positive feeling will be elevated further when you read the next chapter, in which we discuss using cash flow forecasting to assess the future.

4

Forecasting in a Fraction of Time

In this chapter we examine forecasting as a strategic tool for non-profit institutions. Since forecasting and risk management are often linked, we explore what your board needs to understand about forecasting and how it can be accomplished more effectively.

A cash flow forecast is a strategic tool. Any forecast has two dimensions. It incorporates preparation for the future and a willingness to be adaptive in the face of uncertainty. To understand this, it helps to think about strategy for a moment. Strategy, according to the ancient sages, is all about direction. You can advance, hold still, or retreat in the face of any possible choice. The art in strategy is to both prepare for the future and to be flexible in your response to changing circumstances. In spanning the two states of preparation and adaptation, forecasting comes into play. Forecasting provides an opportunity to imagine the future as a form of preparation. It also creates the basis for adaptation, or modifying your approach to fit new or changing circumstances.

By projecting cash flow into the future an organization can forecast its intent in a concrete manner. Forecasts create a sense of the direction the organization is heading. A cash flow forecast is an organizational strategy expressed in numbers. It gives heft to the goals and objectives that the organization adopts and creates measures that can be independently weighed by others.

What can cash flow tell us about the future?

If you can tell the future, or you know someone who can, don't waste your time holding fundraisers. Pick winning lottery numbers or head to the race track and use those sure-fire predictions to buy tickets for long odds on the ponies. The same is true for folks who read tea leaves.

For the rest of the world, forecasting future events in complex systems such as nonprofit organizations is more challenging. As you might expect by now, we believe the key to forecasting is working within a cash flow framework.

In line with our simple and easy theme, we created the software for the *Cash Flow Forecaster* to take some of the hard work out of imagining the future—see the downloadable product described in the Preface. (Ordering information is at www.josseybass.com/go/cashflowsolution.) The Forecaster contains a critical hypothesis, which stems directly from our experience of working with clients over many years. As we assisted clients in creating cash flow budgets, we noticed a pattern with institutions that we worked with year after year. At first it was subtle, but quickly it became apparent to us that the shape of the cash flow curve for any given institution was essentially the same from year to year.

If you stop and think about it, this makes sense. Despite the apparent randomness of grants from donors and foundations, the annual life of a nonprofit institution has a certain seasonality. For example, the school collects tuition for the fall semester during August and September, which results in a spike in income during those months. In May, the big fundraising event brings another surge of income as partygoers dance the night away for goodness knows how much per ticket. The summer is slow, both in income and expense, and then the cycle starts up again. People in the performing arts will recognize the seasonality of subscription campaigns and fund drives at other times. Need we say more than *Nutcracker*?

Just looking at the shape of the curve—with income and expense dancing around the intersection of plus and minus numbers—provides some information, but it does not tell the whole story. The information that is not included is the amplitude of the curve, the degree to which income and expense increase or decrease during any given financial period. In other words, the anonymous donation last year and the sudden increase in heating oil might not be anticipated. But despite these surprises, the overall shape of the curve seems pretty constant from one year to the next for the individual institution. As a result, the cash flow curve can become an important tool for forecasting.

What is special about this electronic Cash Flow Forecaster?

Cash flow forecasting has been around for a long time. It is highly likely that staff members of your institution use a cash flow spreadsheet to project the numbers for future budgets. Cash flow spreadsheets enable you to manipulate and calculate the rows and columns within a budget projection. If you want to explore different projections of income and expense, individual calculations must be performed to see how they unfold over the course of the fiscal year.

The Cash Flow Forecaster is different because it contains algorithms that provide an allocation formula based on our hypothesis about the shape of your institution's cash flow curve. This means that when you introduce assumptions into the Cash Flow Forecaster the entire budget is revised and the graphics enable you to immediately see the impact of your judgment.

For example, let's say that you believe that earned income for next year will increase by 5 percent and that all expenses, including inflation, will increase by 7 percent. By simply dropping those two numbers into the Cash Flow Forecaster you can instantly see the effect on your projected budget.

Given the ease of testing different assumptions, it is possible to quickly generate many different scenarios. You have more choices this way and—since each assumption represents a potential future path—if you monitor your progress through the year, you can assess the accuracy of your financial predictions.

The Cash Flow Forecaster enables you to strike a balance between the inevitable unpredictability of an unknowable future and the need to combine preparation and adaptability in thinking about the future. In this context, preparation is the process of gathering and analyzing financial data to formulate budgets and projections. Adaptability is the process of generating alternative scenarios, some of which may be used to accommodate the institution's strategy to changing circumstances. Classical financial management systems emphasize preparation. In our approach, the emphasis is on adaptability.

The classical approach to forecasting normally contains a highly prescriptive system of fiscal rules and policies. In such a system, it makes good sense to lean on administrative procedures that are tightly linked to the budgetary process. The implicit goal is to muster the resources of the institution in an attempt to obtain precision in forecasting. Nevertheless, most texts still advocate having credit or a cash reserve in place to cover shortfalls and unexpected drops in income or increases in expenses.

Our approach leads to exactly the same place, the use of credit to respond to the unexpected. The difference is that we avoid, consciously, the mustering of significant institutional resources and instead rely on the pattern or curve that is created by actual income and expense figures from the prior year. From our point of view, the ease of using the prior year's actuals and not the prior year's budgeted numbers helps to create a platform from which to move into the future.

To state this in slightly different terms, imagine that you observed all the administrative personnel at a major educational institution, such as Stanford University, participating in their annual planning endeavor. You might see that they were using a planning and budgeting process that was lengthy and time-consuming. When the effort was over, they would undoubtedly have produced a well-informed document effectively allocating resources in the coming year. But would these planning and budgeting efforts be adequate for forecasting?

If you believe that forecasting is largely about preparation, then it is likely that you would believe these efforts will be rewarded. In effect, you are betting on past performance and good planning to prepare for the future. But what really happens?

In a three-year period, Stanford, despite its excellent budgetary planning process and long history of effective fund raising, experienced a series of unanticipated circumstances that in the 2001 fiscal year resulted in the university receiving $120 million less in gifts and grants than in the year 2000. A 26 percent drop in contributions.[5] During the same three-year period Stanford's endowment, one of the largest in the country, took major hits in a sour market, which significantly decreased the amount of investment income available. In 2002, the institution suffered a $17 million deficit, which prompted it to freeze faculty and staff salaries for the coming year.[6]

Knowing all this, suppose you tried to predict the cash flow balance at the end of the year in Stanford's budget three years hence. You would want to know something about the recent income and expense figures from the institution, perhaps from last year. You also might like some information about the characteristic pattern of income and expense in relation to time that constitutes Stanford's cash flow.

This is a function that the Cash Flow Forecaster serves. It automatically supplies an allocation formula about the likely cycle of income and expense over time that characterizes the organization in question, based on last year's actual income and expense. Because it does this with much less informational input, the Cash Flow Forecaster allows you to keep advancing your forecast on a daily, weekly, monthly, or quarterly basis. Since you can easily feed in new information, you are likely to be highly adaptive as conditions change from month to month. In the case of Stanford, the use of a rolling forecast might have allowed the institution to avoid some of the difficulties that it ran into when its budgetary process did not mirror the rapid changes in its environment.

Stanford University is hardly a target for criticism. Rather, its experience, which incidentally is mirrored by many other organizations across the nation in the past three years, may be helpful and instructive.

We hope that this example helps to demonstrate the difference between the conventional approach to forecasting—which calls for a considerable amount of time and energy and tends to lock the institution into a game plan—and our method. By making the process itself simpler and easier through the judicious use of automation and some mathematical concepts, our hope is that institutions can be more adaptive and responsive to changing conditions.

What does all this mean for us, as board members?

The Cash Flow Forecaster enables ordinary people, with diverse levels of skill in financial management, to grasp the notion that it is possible to keep advancing their forecasts and to easily generate new scenarios as a way to be both prepared and adaptive.

How does the Cash Flow Forecaster work in practice?

Here is an example of a nonprofit institution that used a seven-year cash flow forecast to address its financial circumstances. As you will see in Figure 4.1, even having a peek at possible futures can be helpful to board members.

In this seven-year forecast, the organization, a small private school, was anticipating a surge in income in the second year and higher expenses the following year. Then, as the number of students got closer to capacity, the increases in income and expenses were projected to stabilize. What makes this projection valuable is not the accuracy of the numbers, but the ability of the board and staff to quickly see the impact of slight variations in enrollment, or tuition, or heating oil expenses, in relationship to the entire annual

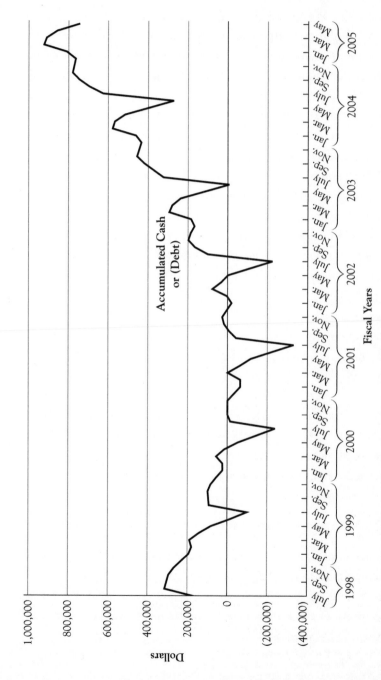

Figure 4.1. Accumulated Cash or (Debt): Seven-Year Forecast.

budget. The Cash Flow Forecaster opens the door to rolling forecasts within which actual income and expense figures can be tracked on a monthly basis and changes made strategically.[7]

It is useful to note that the small private school was able to meet its seven-year projections during a period that was remarkably turbulent for the economy and many nonprofit organizations. By using cash flow as a basic budgetary instrument and the Cash Flow Forecaster as a source of guidance, the institution kept itself in good shape.

The Cash Flow Forecaster allows both large and small organizations to project cash flow. It creates a "fuzzy forecast," one that is useful for dealing with future events. The conventional approach creates what appears to be a precise forecast, yet both approaches are subject to the uncertain nature of the future.

Our intent when forecasting is not to be seduced by the appearance of precision, but rather to become comfortable with the hazy, uncertain nature of the forecast itself. It is essential to remember, as Peter L. Bernstein reminds us: "Anything can happen. We do not and cannot know the future."[8] Yet, as Bernstein also reminds us, "Whether you should take a risk depends not just on the probability that you are right, but also on the consequences if you are wrong." It is the willingness to deal with consequences that makes the board so vital in looking ahead.

These thoughts should help to set your mind at ease about whether the forecaster will pinpoint your exact financial position two years out, to the penny. It will not. What it will do is enable you to quickly revise your forecasts and to immediately see the graphic implications.

What are we to do in the face of an uncertain future?

Once you and your staff members understand the fiscal position of your institution from a cash flow perspective and once you can generate efficient forecasts, the next issue is how to deal with the financial consequences of this new information as you monitor your institution's fiscal reports.

5

Monitoring in Moments

Effective financial management always involves monitoring forecasts and comparing them to last year's figures for income and
expense, or at least comparing last year's actuals to this year's actual
numbers. Yet, of the many chores assigned to board members, it's
probably safe to say that less than a majority (much less, call it 10
percent if you're feeling generous) of all trustees are genuinely
excited about this one. It is the other 90 percent that we were
thinking about when we applied some radical thinking to financial
reports.

In this chapter we examine "the need to know" and how best to
deliver that essential information to the boardroom each month.
We discuss some techniques for weighing financial information and
revisit the virtues of a rolling forecast as a means for using cash flow
to help you manage the institution.

What do board members really need to know when monitoring financial reports?

It is axiomatic that for financial management to be successful, someone has to be minding the store. Counting the beans, along with all
the other items and transactions, the comings and goings, is after
all what taking care of business is all about. But do board members

always have to be the ones counting, or is this a case where a division of labor might be a benefit to everyone?

The answer, we believe, is that board members need to see the big picture, the general direction in which the institution is heading. Boards are asked to make policy, not to mull over every detail in the ledger. Pointing the way for the institution to proceed rarely requires weighing each item on a long budget form against its historical or forecast counterpart.

Board members do need to see whether the institution's monthly income and expenses are significantly different this year from what they were last year. Differences in these overall numbers should then be discussed in the boardroom and decisions made to effect a shift in plans or policies if called for by circumstances.

On the other hand, staff members and their professional financial advisers must pay careful attention to the details, the item-by-item issues that have an immediate impact on operations. If the price of heating oil has suddenly climbed but the price of copier paper has dropped, the staff is meant to assess the impact of these numbers on operations and to make adjustments, in some cases on a daily or weekly basis. The item-by-item approach is a tool for linking actual figures from the past to current figures and taking action where needed.

This differentiation between what the staff needs to know and what the board needs to know may seem uncomfortable to you. Yet imagine a meeting at which a board member spends half an hour pressing the executive director for an item-by-item explanation for why this year's fundraising efforts were below last year's results. And while this was going on, everyone is ignoring the role of inflation on the institution's budget, or the recently published national survey that reported that contributions in this area were 15 percent lower this year than last.

The point is that item-by-item historical variable analysis (a measurement technique that compares past and present numbers

and offers a percentage of variance) may not be the most productive way for board members or staff to spend their time. If you need
specific information, the bookkeeper can provide it in a moment or
two, outside the meeting. In the company of your peers on the
board, your time is better spent concentrating on the overall direction of the organization. We suggest that board members focus on
the big picture and let the staff and their hired financial helpers look
at the item-by-item details.

To push this radical thinking a trifle further, consider a second
component of monitoring, the comparison of last year's actual
figures for income and expense and the forecasts that were em-
bedded in this year's budget. Perhaps you have seen reports that
compare year-to-date budgeted figures with year-to-date actual
figures? Again, it is possible to do a little historical variance analysis to determine the percentage difference.

Say the staff projected a $50,000 grant in March and the check
did not arrive that month. Your variance will be a negative 100 percent. But have you really gained much in terms of real understanding? What you are actually doing is comparing the margin of error
between your staff's forecast and your past experience. You might
hold the director's toes to the fire, but as a board member, what do
you gain by this exercise, other than a loss of confidence in the ability of staff to predict the future?

However, by simply adjusting your monitoring objectives slightly,
you may be able to gather some information that is very appropriate
for the board to contemplate. Imagine walking into the future facing backward. Metaphorically speaking, that is what you do when
you compare your institution's last year's numbers for income and
expense with your forecasts. You are trying to use the past to inform
the future. And while this may be reassuring, as noted in the chapter
on forecasting, it may not always be helpful. Instead, we propose that
you walk into the future facing forward and in the process, create the
rolling forecasts that we discussed earlier.

How can we monitor the fiscal affairs of the organization using a cash flow budget report?

Of the various approaches to monitoring the financial position of nonprofit institutions, perhaps the most common is the use of an item-by-item comparison of last year's financial performance with this year's projected budget figures and with this year's actual figures for income and expense. Variance analysis, as it is called, presents board members with reports that compare these figures, usually expressed as percentages. For example, if heating oil cost $1,500 per month last year, and the staff projected the cost to be $1,600, these two figures can be compared. The change or variance would be reported as 7 percent. But suppose the cost this year is not $1,600 per month. Instead it is $2,100 per month. Then the variance would be closer to 29 percent. For the numerically inclined all this detail may be interesting or even amusing, but what about the rest of the board members? You need to see the big picture, and you need to see it in a hurry. As a result, we propose a different approach.

Rather than sweating the variance between last year's actuals for income and expense, the budgeted figures, plus the difference between the old actuals and the new actuals, we suggest cutting to the chase. Simply report the changes that occur between the projections based on last year's actual income and expense and this year's actual monthly income and expense figures. For the majority of board members monitoring an organization's fiscal affairs, the projected to actual information is enough to work with and the amount of information is much more manageable.

This comparison is easily accomplished by having the bookkeeper place the actual monthly totals for income and expense into the Cash Flow Forecaster. You can instantly see the status of your organization at the end of the month and compare it with your forecast for this period. The Cash Flow Forecaster program automatically recalculates your projections. It reveals the consequences of the actual income and expense and presents the information both numerically and graphically.

Figure 5.1 provides an example that shows an organization that has had a different experience in the month of March than it did the previous year. The graphs instantly reveal a difference for those who are less inclined to spot the numerical differences.

What you are seeing is a direct comparison between the actual figures for the month of March in one year and actual figures for the next year. There was a significant drop in income, from $34,158 in the first year to $17,500 in the next year. Expenses dropped modestly from $39,594 to $36,482, but the overall impact on the institution was substantial.

However, if the forecast that was generated near the end of the last year had projected a likelihood that March might be a month with less income and slightly less expense, the differences would be much smaller, and you could proceed with a sense your forecasts were moving into the future with some confidence. For example, if

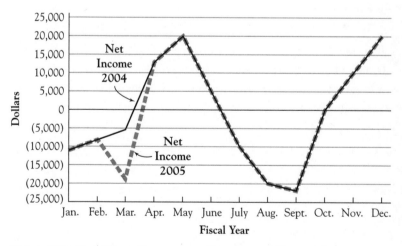

Figure 5.1. Cash Flow Comparison (Income and Expense): 2004 and 2005.

the forecast had projected a drop in income to approximately $20,000, given a shift in funding for a grant from a local foundation, the difference between that figure and the actual income number of $17,500 would be far less surprising.

Are you suggesting that we drop our conventional financial reports?

Absolutely not. Your conventional financial reports play an important role in helping you fulfill your responsibilities as board members. What we are proposing is that you incorporate the cash flow reports into your board meetings and that you use the Cash Flow Forecaster to make everyone's life easier. The seconds it takes the bookkeeper to drop the monthly actuals for income and expense into the Cash Flow Forecaster will enable every board member to quickly grasp the financial position of your institution. Staff will spend less time preparing elaborate reports for the board, although they will still continue to focus on the day-to-day fiscal questions, and your board meetings will be crisper and perhaps even more fun for everyone.

With a cash flow budget, a cash flow forecast, and some ideas for efficient cash flow monitoring, you have a framework within which to employ some very useful analytical tools to financial questions. In the next chapter we offer you a little more advice and some cash flow principles to live by.

6

Cash Flow Analysis and Some Operating Principles

Cash flow analysis opens the door to understanding three key factors in nonprofit financial management:

- The relative cost of funds that are raised, earned, and borrowed

- The role of inflation on budgets

- The importance of time and timing in nonprofit financial governance

In this chapter we examine how these three concepts will help shape your thinking about strategic issues that emerge all the time in the boardroom.

How can cash flow thinking help us evaluate our operational use of money?

Paying careful attention to cash flow introduces the concept of the cost of capital into your financial thinking. In business, the variable cost of money is a primary consideration in many financial decisions. In the nonprofit world, the costs of raising a dollar or earning a dollar or borrowing a dollar are often ignored. Cash flow analysis enables the board to make decisions about which type of capital to use in specific situations. Each dollar, whether raised, or earned, or borrowed, costs a different amount to acquire, and good cash flow management allows the institution to make an informed judgment in its own best interest.

The three types of money available to a nonprofit—funds raised, earned revenue, and the judicious use of credit—all work together, like the three legs of a stool. Take away one and you have a less stable financial platform. Together, the use of gifts and grants, retained earnings, and credit helps your institution deal with the often chaotic financial environment nonprofits confront. The wise use of all three approaches can bring remarkable stability to organizations.

How does the cost of money influence financial decisions?

The first consideration for every nonprofit should be the cost of raising money. While there is considerable speculation within the nonprofit sector about the actual costs of raising funds, one organization that has clearly identified these costs is the Association for Health Care Philanthropy, which has studied the issue for years.[9] Among the group's member institutions, those that have been raising significant sums of money for more than five years spend a median (half above and half below) of 26 cents to raise $1, while those that have been fundraising for less than two years spend a median of 56 cents to raise $1. The major variable in this survey was time.

This actually makes sense. Think about the funding pyramid in which organizations slowly sift and sort through the pool of potential donors to reach the 20 percent of donors who actually give 80 percent of the money. All this effort requires time and money. Gradually, as more large donors are identified, the costs of raising funds from them should decline, since they are a much more targeted audience for fundraising appeals.

In professional development work, the real costs of conducting a long-term campaign, with an annual component, special fund features, and an occasional capital requirement, all have to be accounted for somewhere.

The second consideration for every nonprofit should be the cost of earning money. Just as it costs money to raise money, it also costs money to earn money. In general, we advise our clients to estimate that they will spend between 90 and 99 cents to earn $1—and for some, the costs may be much higher.

By way of example, most American businesses operate with relatively small profit margins. Supermarkets, for example, can spend as much as 98 cents to raise $1 from their customers. Now think about the theater you attend, which prints in each play program, *Your ticket pays for one half of our annual costs.* Which is another way of saying, *We just spent $2 to get your $1 admission.* Not necessarily a good deal, except that foundations, corporations, government agencies, and individual donors are all solicited to make up the balance of the costs through their gifts and grants.

The third consideration is the cost of borrowing. Borrowing, particularly if it is fully secured by collateral that is cash or a cash equivalent, is very inexpensive. Many bankers are willing to lend at or below prime for fully secured nonprofit organizations.

So money costs money, and different types of money—the dollar you raise for gifts and grants, the dollar you earn from sales or services, and the dollar you borrow from a bank—all have different costs. The key to effective money management—in the nonprofit world—is knowing which dollar is most cost-effective for which situation.

How does inflation play into this?

Inflation—the increasing price of goods and services that causes a decline in purchasing power—is a fact of life in American society in the twenty-first century. Although the inflation rate is currently moderate (it averaged 2.5 percent from 1994 through 2005), it still must figure into any nonprofit's fiscal thinking.

The nonprofit sector frequently understates inflation. A fudge factor for *cost of living* may be slipped into the salary and fringe benefits column in the budget for the staff, but across-the-board inflation factors of 5 percent or 6 percent, the actual rate for nonprofits, rarely appear. Nonprofit inflation rates are higher than those of the nation as a whole for three reasons:[10]

- The nonprofit sector is more labor intensive.

- The nonprofit sector lacks economy of scale.

- The nonprofit sector has no incentive to invest in advanced technologies.

One easy way to see the impact of inflation on your institution is to place your best estimate of inflation into the Cash Flow Forecaster under the three-year tab. If you start with last year's actual figures for income and expense, and then project your best estimate of the percentage of inflation for the coming years, the program will project your estimated inflation rate across your budget.

It only takes a second to do this. And seeing the percentage of inflation allocated across the entire budget will provide your board with a new sense of the importance of inflationary trends. Inflation exists; don't ignore it for a moment. When estimating future expense, calculating investment income, and comparing and contrasting the cost of different dollars, inflation must be factored into the equation.

And time?

Time poses a special problem in the nonprofit sector. The funding environment seems chaotic in part because none of the funders, including foundations, corporations, government agencies, or individual donors, coordinate their deadlines or grant periods. Moreover, none of these funders typically ask for cash flow budgets, which integrate money and time. Instead, they ask for balance sheets that provide a fiscal snapshot, or annual budgets that compress an entire year into a single income and expense projection.

Failing to acknowledge the role of time often leads to financial mismanagement of nonprofit organizations. Timing issues—such as not having enough cash on hand to meet payroll when the check from the foundation has not arrived—are frequently defined as fiscal problems in the nonprofit world. Cash flow analysis offers a remedy for this. In case after case, we have found that by using cash flow budgets and forecasts, financial problems can be anticipated and solved quickly. Deficits can be systematically erased, and institutional finances stabilized.

What's the bottom line in all this for our institution?

In business there is one bottom line. You are either fiscally solvent, or you are on the way to being out of business. At least in theory, decisions can be focused on that one bottom line, letting the chips fall where they may.

All nonprofits have two bottom lines: the immediate pursuit of their social or artistic purpose, and long-term fiscal solvency. Social purpose distinguishes nonprofit organizations from commercial entities. In this way, nonprofits are profoundly different from businesses that focus exclusively on being fiscally solvent.

In the nonprofit sector, both bottom lines command our attention, and they often compete. When the artistic director comes forth with a proposal for truly grand costumes for the show, the board may be torn between the budget and the expensive aesthetic vision of the production. Business sense might tell us to pare back the production costs, but our artistic sensibilities may wholeheartedly support the concept of making an opulent statement. This happens all the time in nonprofit organizations, particularly in cultural institutions, and demonstrates the tension between fulfilling the social or artistic mission of the organization and keeping the budget in balance.

If there are two bottom lines in the nonprofit world, how are we supposed to make sound financial decisions?

You and your staff members currently lack reference points within the nonprofit sector that can be used to assess fiscal policies. In the commercial world, a number of key indicators help people see the consequences of their financial policies. Beyond profitability, for-profit leaders can use numerous markers, including markets, to judge their financial decisions. Industry-wide statistics allow for comparison. Analysts study trends and patterns and report on their findings. Data from credit and other services help define levels of performance. For-profits have a wealth of information to use in comparing and contrasting fiscal performance.

Unfortunately, the nonprofit sector has access to very limited data on financial performance. Attempts over the years—by consultants, well-intentioned university professors, and accounting firms—to establish meaningful ratios and other indicators of performance have met with disappointing results. Ratios are at their best when compared to something else. Unfortunately, two major difficulties confront users of ratio analysis in the nonprofit field. One is a lack of standard definitions for various financial terms. The second is a lack of comparable data that makes it difficult to apply "industry" standards when trying to decide whether to go for the expensive production values or to rein in the budget.[11]

Cash flow budgets and reports can help you see the internal workings of your institution. These approaches will assist you in establishing the norms that will characterize your annual cash flow.

Through effective monitoring of financial reports, especially cash flow reports available at each board meeting, your board can stay on top of things. Once your financial picture is clear, it's possible to spot shortfalls before they happen, allowing enough time to put preventive measures into play. On the other hand, seeing potential surpluses allows for a more effective use of capital. Our approach to shortfalls and windfalls is discussed in the next chapter, on financial stability.

Part II

Applying
the Cash Flow Solution

7

Nonprofits and Borrowing Money

In this chapter we take you through the steps necessary to achieve financial stability without large cash reserves or emergency fundraising campaigns. We discuss cash reserves and endowments in later chapters, but for now, our focus is on defining a new resource for you to use so that borrowing can be a financial stabilization strategy.

A key premise of this book is that if you understand your institution's cash flow, you can convert that understanding into a line of credit with your local bank. Borrowing is our metaphor for all the skills necessary to prepare clear and understandable financial statements, to project your cash flow, to forge a working understanding of credit with your board of directors, and to create a community-based creditholders group. It also involves selling the organization and its fiscal position to a possibly reluctant banker.

As disciples of debt, we talk frankly with you about borrowing that is safe and sane. We introduce and define a number of terms related to your use of credit. We discuss creditholders and how they can be a vital asset to your institution, to say nothing of opening the door to the prudent use of credit. Since we urge you to use local banks for your borrowing, we discuss the important steps to follow when you deal with your local banker.

What is the management-by-crisis mode of operating—and how can we avoid it?

The management-by-crisis mode of operating ultimately comes down to not having the funds you need to pay the bills you have, when you need to pay them. Perhaps the single least understood method for stabilizing the financial situation of a nonprofit organization is the use of credit or borrowing. Businesses across America routinely borrow when they need funds and pay back when they don't. Yet for many in the nonprofit sector, borrowing carries with it an undeserved stigma and is viewed as a sign of poor management.

What is a line of credit?

A line of credit is a loan. Like ice cream, loans come in different flavors. Rather than granting a series of operating loans related to specific transactions, the bank may set up a line of credit. In this arrangement, the nonprofit is allowed a bit more freedom, since a set sum has been placed at its disposal, on an annual basis. This means that the institution does not have to relate each borrowing to a single specific purpose; instead, it may use the funds for general, short-term operational needs. Lines of credit come as secured and unsecured agreements. Typically, the line of credit must be repaid for at least thirty days during the yearlong cycle. We advocate that nonprofit organizations provide security for their lines of credit in the form of collateral from creditholders.

Who are creditholders?

To borrow, you need collateral. It's a basic fact of life in the real world. Collateral is something that most nonprofit organizations seem to have in short supply, so we focus on your developing a new category of volunteer in the nonprofit sector, a group of supporters known as creditholders.

The term *creditholder* was coined in an article in the *Practical Philanthropist* in 1992.[12] Creditholders are individuals or institutions that support the mission of a nonprofit organization by providing collateral to a bank. The creditholder's funds—either as cash used to purchase a certificate of deposit at the bank or as stocks and bonds—are pledged as a source of repayment for either a line of credit or for term loans. The creditholders retain ownership of their assets, but make them available to assist the institution. Unlike cosigners, who guarantee repayment of a loan through a promissory note, creditholders are prepared to place a liquid asset in the hands of the bank to serve as collateral.

While we are at it, what is collateral?

Collateral is an asset that is used to offset the risk taken by a lender. Collateral comes in various forms, but for our purposes we are talking about collateral as cash or cash equivalents. Collateral is normally required until a loan is repaid. In the event of default, the lender has a legal right to claim the collateral as payment of the loan.

What is hypothecation?

Hypothecation means that you are pledging an asset to a lender but not relinquishing control over that asset. So creditholders *hypothecate* assets when they buy a certificate of deposit or pledge shares of stock or a bond as collateral. The collateral allows your nonprofit institution to borrow. The key point is that the creditholder does not lose control over the asset; it still remains the creditholder's property unless the nonprofit defaults on its obligation.

What are term loans?

A term loan has a maturity in excess of one year. Term loans offer some advantages to the borrower. The installment repayment schedule and the amount of payment are usually tailored to fit the borrower's financial activities. In the nonprofit sector, term loans can be used to address deficits, if they are fully secured. The length of time needed to repay the loan gives the institution an opportunity to slowly and in some cases gracefully meet its obligations.

———————

With these terms in mind, addressing the challenge of financial stability is simple, once you have mastered cash flow budgeting, monitoring, and forecasting.

Can the bank lend to us without collateral?

Bankers cannot lend to you without collateral, except under special circumstances that typically require community service loans to be given a special high-risk designation. Nonprofit organizations trying to establish a line of credit discover that banks require two guarantees of repayment—cash from operations and assets to act as collateral—before they are willing to lend. Typically, the primary source of repayment is from a nonprofit's earnings or from grants and gifts. The real problem for many institutions is that they lack assets that bankers can easily convert into cash, which means they lack collateral.

Collateral, collateral, who's got the collateral?

If we think of collateral as the closets of old roller skates donated in 1889 for the orphans, or the dozens of boxes of chalk and cracked blackboards in the old one-room schoolhouse, then nonprofits are in trouble. Very few bankers want reams of used file folders, or donated computers that run seven-inch disks, or a performing arts center with a leaking roof and a failing furnace.

You, however, do have access to a form of collateral that you may not have considered—one that is within your reach and one that bankers worldwide are happy to accept without reservation. After all, bankers have fantasies, too. What bankers dream about, when they imagine the most perfect collateral in the world, is cash, plain old-fashioned cold, hard cash. And you have access to cash and very liquid cash equivalents (stocks and bonds) from the people who support your organization. This cash is provided by creditholders and it is the collateral that always enables you to borrow.

All nonprofit organizations need a creditholders group. Creditholders are the people who love you. They are the people you will grow to love. They support your mission. In some cases they may be the people you serve, or perhaps their parents or grandparents. Creditholders are friends, associates, supporters, family members, staff members, alumni, former patients, ex-addicts who have gone on to be rock stars or motivational speakers, or almost any other constituent. These are the people who help by placing an amount of their savings into a special interest-bearing account at the bank.

Usually, these funds are used to purchase a certificate of deposit. The money in the account is pledged to the bank as collateral for borrowing by the nonprofit. Each creditholder receives interest based on the amount on deposit. Interest is paid out annually or rolled over into the account.

Some creditholders have stocks or bonds they use in place of cash. In this case the bank holds the certificates, often discounting the total value of the stocks, since bankers recognize that stocks rise and fall, even if other people don't always believe this is true.

Speaking of ups and downs, what about risk?

By now you have a cash flow budget, or at least the understanding of how to set one up, and you have the Cash Flow Forecaster that can act as your slightly cloudy crystal ball. You can see your cash flow, the influx of income and the outflux of expenses. Remember the graphic images in the Cash Flow Forecaster; they enable you to project the times when you need to borrow and the times when you have the funds to pay back the bank. In other words, you have a pretty clear sense of when you need help and when you don't.

All this poses very little risk to the creditholders. However, before soliciting funds from creditholders for a line of credit, it is helpful if your board establishes a policy stating that the line of credit will be used only to cover fluctuations in cash flow, not to address long-term debt or to serve as venture capital. (Later we talk about establishing a different set of policies for long-term borrowing, but for now it's best to stay with the specific use of a line of credit to flatten out your cash flow peaks and valleys.)

This means that before the creditholders' funds are pledged as collateral, the institution will already have determined its capacity to repay the loan from operational funds. Given this policy, the degree of risk to creditholders is kept very low. You and your board should talk face-to-face with people about becoming creditholders based on your cash flow forecasts. You should explain how their dollars will help you borrow from the bank during those periods when you are low on cash.

After you explain the organization's borrowing policy and outline any possible risks, each person can be asked to place a modest sum into a collateral account. Our rule of thumb here is that creditholders should never pledge more cash than they are willing to lose if something untoward happens. For this reason, it typically makes sense to have lots of creditholders who all feel safe and understand that everyone is sharing the risks. Losses happen in an uncertain world, even to the best of people, with the best of motives, in the safest of situations.

Say, have you checked out interest rates of late?

The incentive of creditholders to support the organization is hardly financial. After all, people can earn interest with complete security in a bank savings account. And even after the Federal Reserve loosens its death grip on interest rates, this is not going to be about making money. Rather, by placing their funds in a special account with your organization's bank, your creditholders will each be helping you operate effectively and furthering the social purpose of your organization, at no cost to themselves. This is particularly true of folks with stocks and bonds.

Is this really legal?

Having creditholders offer cash or cash equivalents to provide the basis for borrowing is legal. Banks have been accepting the pledge of financially valuable items as security without transferring possession or title for a long, long time.

As a cautionary note, it is always wise to tread carefully before adopting a new financial approach. Having said that (our lawyers can now relax), obviously, it makes sense to check with your lawyer to ensure that no state laws are violated. To date, creditholders groups have encountered no legal obstacles that we or our lawyers are aware of, but it is still wise to check out your local situation before proceeding.

How does a creditholders group offer advantages to us, to themselves, and to our bank?

With a creditholders group, your organization gains a stable resource that can be used to mobilize credit whenever it can be shown that other sources of revenue will repay the loan. Interest charged by banks for lines of credit secured by creditholders' certificates of deposit are typically one to two points above the interest paid by the bank for the certificates of deposit. This is often below prime rate.

Borrowing at a lower rate enables nonprofits to pay their vendors quickly, gain discounts, and avoid late-payment penalties. When vendors are asked to provide donations rather than discounts for fast payment, their response is usually to contribute slightly more, often offsetting the interest costs of borrowing.

Creditholders gain an opportunity to provide invaluable assistance to a nonprofit organization they believe in, without cost to themselves. And the bank gains the collateral it needs to justify a loan to the organization.

Why go through all this bother? Why not just ask for donations, create a cash reserve, and call it a day?

This is a valid question. But before we answer it, here is a quick definition for a cash reserve. *Cash reserves* are sums of money that are used in the nonprofit and in the commercial sector, dedicated to the purpose of meeting current and future obligations. Cash reserves are similar to savings accounts, in the sense that since they are often needed on short notice, they are highly liquid (meaning they can be quickly converted into cash), as in a bank savings account or a mutual fund that allows for easy withdrawal. Normally cash reserves earn low rates of interest, given their low risk and high liquidity.

The answer is that, while donations are still important and will be gratefully accepted, your organization may have ongoing cash flow requirements that need to be addressed. At current levels of fundraising, and with earned revenue that may be just able to support the existing operations, stabilizing cash flow is an essential component of good management. Placing money in the creditholder pool will help ensure the long-term survival of the institution by enabling it to handle its current obligations gracefully and still present excellent programs or services. Also, remember that money costs money and the cost to your institution of creating a cash reserve is a factor that must be considered.

Are there really things that can go bump in the night?

As practitioners, we have seen some very strange things in the nonprofit world. So it comes as no surprise to us that the way institutions set up creditholder programs isn't always "by the book." Of course, we hope that people will follow our advice and that they will take our recommendations seriously and literally, but that is not always the case.

So long as there are human beings, there will be problems with any social endeavor, including creditholder programs established by nonprofit institutions. Here are some of the problems that we have observed over the past thirty years:

In some cases not enough board and staff members were willing to commit to the creditholder program. So, even though the organization brought the cost of participation down to a level that meant everyone could subscribe, only a few individuals signed up. These enrolled creditholders were in effect being asked to carry more than their fair share of the burden. Without adequate support, the creditholder program could not get off the ground.

The lesson here is that if your board decides to start a creditholder program, urge every member to participate. Plan to fully subscribe the program and don't stop recruiting creditholders until you have reached your goal.

Then there is the borrowing that is not fully secured by creditholders. Acquiring debt as a new resource can be very exciting, but it is imperative that everyone on the board understand both its positive and negative consequences. Borrowing that is fully secured provides day-to-day funds as a resource in which the risk has been spread among many different participants. By providing a dollar of collateral for every dollar that is borrowed, the board and staff can make sure that debt will be used responsibly.

Why pay interest to the bank when we could just handle this ourselves?

Saving interest is always on people's minds. Yet in this case, the marginal cost of interest provides the institution with an everyday resource and a highly dependable, emotionally detached banker who can be counted on to make careful decisions that reinforce the financial health of the organization.

And speaking of banks—if you have warmed to the idea of using credit to help to create financial stability for your organization, then the next section on dealing with your banker when you have a creditholder program will be a real eye-opener.

8

Meeting Your Banker

Talk of credit always makes us think of bankers, and well it should. Banks, not foundations, are really where the money is. And this is particularly true on the local level. Many small communities, even those that lack foundations or other institutional funders, have banks. Banks and bankers will never look the same to you after reading about how helpful they can be if you have the right stuff to share with them.

In this section we offer a rationale for heading to your local bank. We discuss the information, financial and otherwise, needed for a visit to the bank. We sketch out for you what is likely to happen when you sit down with your local banker for both the first and second meetings. And we offer a few hints to make your loan shopping experience more fun.

Why banks?

Many people maintain that in the nonprofit sector loans should come from special programs at foundations, such as program-related investment funds (PRIs), or from special financial organizations set up to serve the special needs of nonprofit institutions. We recommend that you think first of going to the bank. And why banks? Well, as the famous bank robber Willie Sutton put it so well, "Because that's where the money is."

Banks are typically local entities. Most communities that are large enough to have nonprofit organizations also have a bank nearby. This is not true of foundations, government agencies, or nonprofit loan funds.

We have a creditholders group; now how do we approach the bank for a line of credit?

Your staff has prepared your annual cash flow budget, complete with footnotes. You have convinced your fellow trustees to institute a creditholders group. They have agreed to make their own funds available and to get others, including staff and other supporters, to participate. You are able to quickly determine the amount of money you need to borrow by looking at your cash flow budget and noting the largest negative monthly figure in the running total.

How do we prepare before we meet the bank?

Only death, pestilence, and taxes inspire as much fear as visits to the bank to ask for money. So you and your designated staff member will want to sit down with your finance committee chair or your board treasurer and review the financial statements that need to be presented to the bank. This is the time to quickly sketch out a strategic plan, a marketing plan, and a brief description of how your institution will pay for expenses in the coming year. These need not be exhaustive planning efforts, but they do need to accurately reflect your best thinking at the time.

This preliminary work will pay a handsome dividend to your institution in the future, not only at the bank but in your fundraising efforts and in your day-to-day operations. Organizations using a consultant to assist them in preparing these materials have found that costs for the service are normally quite modest.

When all your homework is done, you will have the following useful insights:

- A clear idea of how much you want to borrow

- Financial reports and plans to repay the loan

- A creditholders group in place and ready to help out

- Enough funds to match the amount you wish to borrow, plus a little extra to allow individual creditholders to pull out their funds in an emergency

In sum, you are ready to go shopping for a bank that will recognize your worth, offer you good terms, and work with you to meet your credit needs in the coming years.

How do we make a date with the bank?

Start by calling the bank where you normally do business. Ask to set up an appointment with a loan officer and indicate that you are interested in establishing a line of credit. Don't be surprised if you encounter some resistance from the people at the bank. A remarkable number of bankers have no idea that nonprofits qualify for, and can use, a line of credit. They may think that you are looking for a donation or an unsecured loan.

What's going to happen at our first meeting?

This depends on the banker, but don't count on too much. The first meeting with your banker should be viewed as a get-acquainted session, with a specific request for a line of credit and some paperwork for the banker to review. Your banker will want to learn more about what you do, your mission, and your program. In addition, your banker will be concerned with how the loan can be repaid, and will want to evaluate your current financial position, your prospects for the future, and the quality of your management. All perfectly normal questions for someone renting money.

When meeting with your banker, the following items are helpful to take along:

Financial statements

- A balance sheet, an income and expense statement, and a schedule of accounts payable and receivable.

- A current annual cash flow budget, with plenty of footnotes.

- A cash flow forecast that looks ahead a couple of years. The forecast will reveal your projected cash flow. The cash flow forecast is especially useful in identifying whether you will have sufficient cash to repay the loan.

- Three years of financial statements if you have been around that long; if not, your creditholders' cash will still ensure a warm welcome at the banker's door.

- The tax form that many nonprofits file, called a 990, should also be included in your package.

Organizational plans

- Strategic financial plan demonstrating the fit between the organization and its environment.

In plain English, it is helpful to have a clue or two about how you are pursuing your mission and how your program or programs relate to the wider world in which you are operating. Placing this information in written form will assist bankers who need to get to know you better. Using the exercises in The Money Matters Kit, your board and staff can quickly and inexpensively create a strategic financial plan that will be helpful to you and to your banker. (The Money Matters Kit can be obtained by contacting www.linzerconsulting.com.)

Okay, we have the paperwork, now what?

Be prepared to answer questions, but remember that you have no need to be defensive. The bank is renting money, and has a right to make sure that you understand your responsibility to repay it. However, you are offering cash as a source of collateral—through your creditholder account—so the banker should be prepared to offer excellent terms on your line of credit, since the bank has no risk associated with your loan.

If you feel uncomfortable during this transaction, tell the banker. You are offering the bank an opportunity to earn income on your borrowing with virtually no risk, and you should be treated very well. If the experience or the terms do not suit you, consider going to another bank. Businesses shop around for banks all the time. While the products offered are pretty much the same, the treatment and service provided vary greatly.

Is it more wonderful the second time around?

There may be many more details to discuss at your second meeting with the banker. Here are some examples:

- What is a fair rate of interest to be charged for borrowing on the line of credit, particularly given the low level of risk to the bank?

- What are the upfront fees and the renewal fees for setting up and maintaining a line of credit? Remember that both are often at the discretion of the lender.

- Will the line of credit grow with your annual budget after the initial year?

- Discuss whether the amount that can be drawn at any given time is a function of the organization's receivables—for example, a percentage of what's owed the organization at any given time. Some bankers want to ensure that their line of credit is not being used to fund an organization's debt, but rather its cash flow. In this case, the lender may tie the line to receivables due in no more than ninety days.

- Does the bank want to have receivables assigned to it for collection? For example, should you send a grant from a government agency directly to the bank as repayment for borrowing?

Can we just sign up for financial stability?

Only after these thorny questions have been resolved will you be prepared to sign up for a revolving line of credit with your bank. After securing your line of credit, make sure you leave a little time to celebrate. You will have achieved a significant milestone in the financial management of your organization. From now on you will have funds available to you to meet your cash flow requirements. Late checks from foundations or government agencies will no longer result in anxious moments as payday approaches. You will have access to a resource that is renewable for as long as you fulfill your end of the bargain.

9

Dealing with Deficits and Other Surprises

Deficits happen. (For the literal minded, we are using the terms *deficit* and *shortfall* interchangeably. We are not referring to the national budget.) In other words, deficits or shortfalls are the financial position an institution finds itself in when it lacks the cash to cover all its current expenses. This may be during the fiscal year or at periodic intervals, but the effect is the same: the rent does not get paid if the organization has no unrestricted money in the checking or savings account.

So an unforeseen event has happened and you discover that you have a deficit. Even though you, as a board member, may have been very vexed by the report at the last meeting about the big shortfall, there is a right way and a wrong way to go about solving the problem.

In this section we offer you some alternatives to that timeworn standby: *off with their heads*. And in the interests of being civil, if not happy, we hope that you will consider adopting more moderate measures. These include finding out why the problem occurred in the first place, then putting into place a term loan, one that extends for more than a year, to allow you time to solve the problem. We also explore some alternative measures, such as emergency fundraising campaigns and cost-cutting tactics. And we talk briefly about the psychological challenge of acknowledging shortfalls in the public arena.

We have suddenly discovered a huge deficit. Before we burn the executive director at the stake and explore Chapter 11 proceedings, is there anything we can do?

Before running for the firewood and matches, you need to correct or take care of the problem created by the deficit, and you need to do it in the way that is least harmful to the organization. Shakespeare was wrong: Hell hath no fury like a *board member* who feels betrayed by suddenly learning of a deficit. Be gentle; find the least painful way to solve the immediate financial problem, and at the same time begin to put into place or refine systems designed to prevent a similar situation from arising in the future.

For heaven's sake, what do we do then?

Even before the bleeding has been stopped, it makes sense to carefully explore the reasons that the deficit occurred. Has it been growing for some time? Given the vagaries of fiscal reporting in many nonprofit organizations, things could have been cooking for a while before anyone smelled the smoke. Look first to the financial reports. Do they reveal a problem? Often a trend has been in the making, but it was not candidly disclosed to the board or was ignored.

Does the deficit follow Linzer's Law of Littles? To wit, did lots of little items, such as small losses of income or small extra expenditures, come together to form a sizable deficit? If things are subtle, with two bottom lines to address, small items can gradually create big deficits. One answer is to refocus in just the opposite way, to look carefully at the big picture.

Return to an examination of cash flow on a monthly basis, looking at total income, total expense, and the running or cumulative total. These numbers can often help to point out when things started going south.

Does the deficit result from the postpartum letdown that accompanies or follows an ambitious capital campaign? Over the years, we can't tell you how many times we've heard board presidents or executive directors moan about the deficit in operating income that hit just after a capital campaign. You are trying to feed two mouths when you raise capital, and without tremendous effort, the operational budget—the daily grind that no one loves to contribute to—will come back to haunt you. Beware the capital campaign: it can be a real deficit maker!

Did someone really make off with the funds?

Is there an address in Bora Bora where you could send a note inquiring about the loss? This sounds funny, but it isn't. Most people who work for nonprofit organizations may be devoting themselves to the public good and social purpose, but some still harbor felonious tendencies. The commercial world is not the only place where people embezzle funds. Good controls and commonsense ideas, such as separating the function of opening the mail from the task of posting checks to the account, can help. Trust us; even though the accountants remain one step behind the crooks, they still have excellent advice to give in this department.

Well, our balance sheet looks fine, so what's the problem?

We have already touched on the distorting effect that restricted funds can have on the institutional bottom line. But it's worth mentioning that many board and staff members fail to spot a cash flow problem because the only financials they are looking at reflect assets and liabilities. When this happens, individuals frequently cannot accept the fact that they glossed over the bad news when it was reported to them. As the saying goes, "Denial is more than a river in Egypt."

Are you suggesting more debt?

Yes, but first try to look calmly at the deficit. How big is it? Do you really understand what caused it to happen? For organizations that assess their financial shortfall as being acute and therefore highly situational, a conventional credit instrument such as a term loan may be appropriate.

Shortfalls happen, often for reasons beyond an organization's immediate control. The weather was terrible and no one came to the major fundraising event, the political party in power got booted and the new guys closed the state agency that provided core funding, or an innocent mistake by the bookkeeper was missed by the auditor and there is less money in the bank than anyone thought. In cases like these, it is important for everyone to slow down and try to look calmly at the deficit. If that is not possible, bring in an outsider, a professional with no stake in the outcome. That person can examine the situation objectively and perhaps unlock the mystery of whether this deficit is an anomaly or a long-standing problem that has just surfaced this year.

It is important to honestly gauge the magnitude of the deficit. How big is it? Could it be brought under control if converted to term debt and paid off, just like a mortgage, over five or more years with reasonable interest payments?

The advantage of term debt when you have a deficit is that it allows you to slowly and deliberately pay off your obligation. The obvious disadvantage is that your deficit may be an indication of underlying operational problems that need to be resolved before you can make money in the future. The board needs to make this determination. The board also needs to put together enough collateral to persuade the bank that it will be protected if it rents you money over a longer period of time.

As a first step, board members may want to establish an internal creditholders group before reaching out to the community. The board members are liable for the financial well-being of the organization. It makes good sense that they would step in first to provide collateral. By offering the banker a liquid asset to collateralize the term loan, they are shouldering the responsibility for curing the problems that caused the deficit. However, once the board has committed some assets to the long-term effort, it is entirely appropriate for the board and staff to reach out to the community for additional creditholders.

After analyzing their situation, many of our clients have repositioned their deficit with their banks. Having a fully secured line of credit already in place means that they have some borrowing history with the bank. This foresighted use of credit saves time and energy when attempting to obtain a long-term loan.

Shouldn't we embark on a massive fundraising effort to cure the accumulated deficit that has recently come to light?

The prospect of going further into debt seems like a lousy idea to many board members. But doesn't it make sense to first ask why you waited until accumulating a deficit to embark on a massive fundraising campaign? If your fiscal reporting did not warn you that a problem was accumulating, that should be a real concern and needs to be addressed. Then, after examining the problem, it may make much more sense to translate the deficit into term debt and develop a strategy to pay it off over time. Some organizations have found that crisis-driven fundraising—the kamikaze approach to development efforts—will work in the short run, but that it is hard to sustain the momentum over the long haul. Fundraising needs to be viewed as a disciplined, ongoing activity, not the end product of poor financial monitoring and inadequate planning for the credit needs of the organization.

Why not just cut everything and save the money?

Generally, when boards are confronted with a deficit at the end of the fiscal year, they respond in one of these ways:

- Institute an emergency fundraising effort.

- Cut the budget by trimming expenses in an attempt to avoid carrying the shortfall forward into the next fiscal year.

- Try to both increase revenues and cut expenses.

In the first case, raising money on an emergency basis will probably take more time than anticipated, and may completely interfere with the operations of the institution. Fundraising typically takes time, if the sums are large, and that means a slow response to an immediate situation.

The second case—a short-term solution of slashing expenses—will immediately solve the shortfall problem but may have serious consequences as program capacity is diminished. The long-term effect of a slash-and-burn policy may be difficulty in obtaining institutional support or donor contributions as programming levels are reduced through austerity.

The third course of action is a combination of cuts in expenses and increasing revenues through fundraising efforts. While it is true that some trimming may be useful, it should be done thoughtfully. Similarly, raising additional funds is always a good idea, although you must be careful to avoid stepping on your own ongoing fundraising requirements.

What this comes down to is a policy that weighs short-term action against long-term results. The one common denominator is that all three tactics are inherently time-based. You need to examine the relationship between time and money, since lack of time, not lack of money, is often the problem that nonprofit organizations face.

Nonprofits don't go bankrupt, do they?

Compared to businesses, which have a high failure rate, relatively few established nonprofit organizations actually go out of business. Instead, they may shrink into smaller and smaller versions of themselves, or they may translate their mission into another social purpose. So, for example, an agency that was set up specifically to assist immigrants from a particular religious, racial, or ethnic group may simply move on to assist members of another group as the original immigrants become settled and no longer need assistance.

This cheery note notwithstanding, some organizations do go out of business. The question that members of the board must ask themselves when contemplating this possibility is whether they will be better served by dealing with an institutional lender in working out the obligations of the organization, or with an assortment of creditors who, in their genuine anxiety about competing with each other for what is left of the funds, may rush to litigate. In other words, the fear of bankruptcy should not dissuade you from considering borrowing as a tool.

If our organization gets into financial trouble, shouldn't some members of the board lend the organization money out of their own pockets?

Whatever the reason for the deficit, well-intentioned board members will often step forth and offer to lend the institution money to get it over the hump created by the deficit. We suggest that you decline this offer, even though it is a wonderful gesture and probably a heartfelt one to boot. The reason for saying no is actually heartfelt, too.

We suggest that board members not lend funds to their organization. Their relationship with the institution is much too important to be cluttered up with personal issues regarding its financial situation. In our experience, board members who lend money often propose the most draconian austerity measures when times are tough for the institution, sometimes to their own and the organization's detriment. Board members can donate money, help with fundraising, pledge funds as collateral, and get others to join you. All these are positive acts. Let the bankers lend, stop worrying about the marginal cost of interest, and get on with the business of the organization with a clear conscience.

My business could not survive if it ran out of money each year, so how can our nonprofit endure these losses?

Deficits are not losses. At least not in the sense of losses in the commercial world. In business, at the end of the year, a company tallies up its receipts and its disbursements and, if there is greater expense than income, declares a loss. This declaration has enormous implications for dividends paid out, for the reputation of the company, for stockholder satisfaction, and for the public assessment of the value of the company, and it has real tax consequences. This is so because distribution is an essential component of any commercial entity.

But for nonprofits, a deficit is often just a shortfall of funds at a moment in time. It may have absolutely no adverse meaning for the long-term health of the organization. For example, an organization with cash-based accounts ends its fiscal year with a check from a major funder in the mail, but not in hand. The deficit is recorded, but two days later the check arrives and no financial crisis occurs.

Because a nonprofit is a pure cash-flow entity, a shortfall sends confusing signals to commercially oriented participants, even if it may actually pose no great threat to the organization—that is, if a method can be embraced that will deal with the deficit, buy time, and allow for analysis of the shortfall and the adoption of measures to address the deficit. Our approach is to urge setting up a credit-holder fund as a source of collateral to establish term debt and to help the organization to get on with its mission.

Won't our golden reputation be ruined by any public discussion of our shortfall?

Shortfalls happen from time to time, even in the best-managed organizations. Over and over we have encountered board and staff members affiliated with an institution that has incurred a shortfall who genuinely believe that they must fix the problem before they tell anyone about it. They apparently believe the problem will stain their reputation in the community or among funders, and therefore must be kept secret or disguised in some other fashion for as long as possible.

Financial difficulties spark powerful emotional reactions. There is blame and shame, to say nothing of guilt and anger. Some directors react by hectoring the board to get out there and raise more money. Others combine this tactic with draconian measures to create austerity. Others weep and offer themselves up to the community as victims of circumstance, and everyone assumes the worst possible consequences.

Perhaps the worst thing that you can do is to feel ashamed of the shortfall. The best thing that you can do is to assess the damage, develop some plausible multiple-year forecasts and plans for resolving the problem, and, if you haven't already done so, schedule an appointment with your banker.

Please tell us we don't have to tell our banker!

For many board and staff members, going to the bank in the midst of a financial crisis seems like exactly the wrong thing to do. People seem to believe that the banker will ask lots of probing questions that will embarrass everyone—and will then take the information, turn you down flat, and write a note to the bank's contributions committee suggesting that your organization be permanently removed as a candidate for corporate grants. It's a pretty grim picture, all in all.

Happily, it's not true. Remember, your organization is going to provide the banker with a dollar of collateral for every dollar that you borrow, over the life of the loan. You have completely removed the downside risk from the banker. As long as your collateral is liquid and the bank is assured of repayment, the banker will not only be your professional friend, in our experience, but will work with you to assess your situation, weigh your assumptions constructively, and in many cases offer a host of nonfinancial forms of assistance.

After all, you do not have to sell the banker on the idea of lending you fully secured funds. That is what banks do for a living. All those multiple-year cash-flow forecasts and plans are designed to convince you, your staff, your board, your creditholders, and your donors that you are viable and going to be all right in the end. It is you, not the banker, who must be comfortable and sure that your plans will work.

10

Capital Accumulation, the Great American Dream

In a magic moment at last night's board meeting, you were delighted to learn that your organization had a surplus for the past year and a retiring board member has just given you a very large unrestricted gift as a parting gesture. Your peers on the board were excited, and there was giddy talk about setting up a cash reserve, or creating an endowment, or even kicking off a capital campaign for a new building.

Endowments, cash reserves, big buildings, and piles of shiny new equipment are all part of the great American dream. And so why not take the surplus in the bank account and treat yourself to one or more of the good things of organizational life?

In this chapter we show you the downside of capital accumulation strategies. We explore some of the financial implications of building and sustaining a cash reserve and an endowment. We share a little math with you on both and cite some sources that suggest that capital accumulation is not helping the institutions who hoard, their constituents, or their communities. Finally, we show you a safe and sane way to get more mission with less money in the coffers.

Americans have always accumulated capital. Why shouldn't we try for it?

Capital accumulation is the name of the game in American fundraising circles today. Many nonprofit organizations are focusing on donations to build cash reserves, endowments, and capital building campaigns in the hope of securing financial stability tomorrow—and taking advantage of the interest among donors in making such gifts today.

But like the grapes hanging on the trellis in Aesop's classic fable about the fox, these acquired funds can remain tantalizingly out of reach for day-to-day operations. The balance sheet may look good, but the actual cash available for running the organization is often surprisingly small.

Despite the popularity of capital accumulation among nonprofits, growing evidence indicates that it is harmful for individual institutions, the constituencies they serve, the local community, and ultimately the entire nonprofit sector. Larger institutions worry about having adequate resources, but the ways in which they handle the money that they acquire is often very inefficient. As a consequence, these institutions offer fewer services relative to their resource base. At the same time, the larger institutions' need for more money, in the face of a relatively inelastic pool of funds, squeezes smaller, less well-endowed institutions.[13]

We want an endowment, a healthy cash reserve, a new building of our own, and lots of equipment; why rain on our parade?

The 1998 report issued by the Statistics on Income Division of the Internal Revenue Service examines the income and asset allocation in the nonprofit sector over the preceding two decades.

The IRS figures demonstrate that giving across the United States is remarkably constant. The pool of grants and donated dollars is fixed or relatively stable. The amount of money contributed each year has grown at slightly less than the rate of inflation. This is true if you consider income from all sources, including individuals, corporations, and government agencies. The overall pool of resources remained constant, in part, because some years corporations and government gave less and in others individual donors were less generous.

To compound this problem, the IRS statistics reveal that financial assets in the nonprofit sector are being accumulated to a remarkable degree, rather than spent on mission. The fourfold increase in the book value of assets is a telling sign of this accumulation. In some fields, such as education and health care, revenues have increased dramatically over two decades, but in other sectors, such as social service and the arts and humanities, revenues have not increased nearly as much. In the years since the IRS study, the trend is upward. In other words, more money is being accumulated than spent in the nonprofit sector.

There is an obvious skew in the size of nonprofits and the assets they hold. If the largest organizations—5 percent of all nonprofits—hold 89 percent of the assets of the sector and derive 80 percent of the total income each year, that leaves 20 percent for the remaining 95 percent of the organizations.

Finally, although foundation assets have increased more than fourfold, the actual percentage of grants, as a function of total assets, has declined significantly. More money is being held; less is being granted.

Since the pie is relatively fixed, the issue becomes one of either finding ways to make each piece go further or having an increasing number of agencies and organizations go hungry.

You can see the problem. The biggest institutions are going to grow. This is true even when these large institutions employ their capital inefficiently with endowments, cash reserves, buildings, and equipment. They will constantly need more funds just to meet their inflation-driven operating expenses. What this means within a community is that the smaller organizations will be starved for resources as their larger peers continue to consume more and more capital. If the pool of resources does not increase, the competition will increase and further disadvantage the smaller institutions.

Not a pretty picture, but it is what happens when institutions accumulate large amounts of money, invest it for long-term gain, yet still have to compete for the remaining scarce resources to satisfy their current requirements.

What's the other side of the coin with regard to endowments?

An endowment is an irrevocable trust. In a legally binding agreement, funds are given to an institution with the understanding, in most cases, that the principal is to be maintained in perpetuity. Only a portion of the income earned can be spent. What this means in practice is that the interest earned is divided into two categories. The first category of money is used to pay for investment advice and money management, for the costs of administration at foundations or financial service companies; and a percentage, usually equal to a three-to-five year rolling average of estimated inflation, is put back into the investment pool to make sure the buying power of the fund lasts forever. The second category is what is left over. This is the money that is disbursed as grants or spent as investment income.

In addition, institutions accumulate capital through cash reserves and funds restricted by the board, often called quasi-endowments. A quasi-endowment is capital held in a cash reserve with the funds restricted by the board. It is actually an internally controlled cash reserve, with a fancy name.

As we mentioned earlier, nonprofits have two bottom lines: the immediate pursuit of their social purpose, and long-term fiscal solvency. An endowment is a financial device that defers the immediate gratification of current operational needs for the imagined long-term benefits of fiscal solvency. The financial strategies that organizations adopt, including endowments or lines of credit, are simply ways to confront the need to deal with financial solvency over time.

Endowments are very popular. Almost everyone in the nonprofit sector wants an endowment, a cash reserve, or a capital campaign to construct a new building or to renovate existing space. In other words, board and staff members are pursuing strategies to accumulate capital for their institutions. Yet endowments are rarely an efficient way to address issues of fiscal solvency. They are costly to raise and contribute relatively little to the annual budget.

Many privately held endowments in this nation spend less than 5 percent each year to fulfill the mission of their organization. In this day of 3 percent inflation, if we add the additional two points that inflation in the nonprofit world is assumed to have, you can see that even at 5 percent, the endowments barely contribute enough to match current inflation, to say nothing of operational needs. If inflation increases again, despite the efforts of the Federal Reserve, the performance of endowments will decline even further.

But won't we be able to borrow against our endowment in times of need?

Probably not. An irrevocable trust (an endowment) is frequently useless in the face of fiscal crisis. You can't touch the principal, and neither can your banker, so you can't borrow by using it for collateral. For this reason, it is technically possible for a nonprofit organization to be, at the same moment, fiscally solvent (at least on paper) and bankrupt. Since you can spend only a portion of the interest, you may have an impressive endowment, but you won't be able to mobilize the money to pay your bills. In this case, interestingly enough, the courts will not liquidate the endowment. Instead, they will transfer the principal to another nonprofit institution, leaving trustees still on the hook to creditors.

If the pool is constant, isn't that all the more reason to get in there and get our share for an endowment?

Inefficient use of funds harms everyone: the institution, the community, and the clients and constituents of nonprofit organizations. When excess funds are devoted to endowments, less money is available to meet the organization's operational needs. This means that clients and constituents receive less service or have to pay a higher price.

In addition to endowments, restricted funds, and cash reserves, capital can also be accumulated in the form of buildings and equipment. The ownership of property and tangible goods is very much part of the tradition of the nonprofit sector, as discussed in the next chapter. We also believe this use of capital is inefficient.

Hey, hold on there. If endowments are so bad, why does Harvard have a $25 billion-plus endowment fund?

It's true that Harvard has an endowment fund that runs to multiple billions—but the fact that many institutions have endowments doesn't mean they are good. To the contrary, endowments are a highly inefficient use of capital, and that is bad.

When an organization decides to accumulate capital, it is choosing to trade current pursuit of its mission for the illusion of future financial security. To accumulate capital for an endowment or other reserve funds, established nonprofit organizations spend money to raise contributions. The money raised generally is then invested conservatively. Inflation and endowment terms dictate that a certain amount be put back into the principal for the endowment to maintain its purchasing power. Taking these factors together, it is clear why the future yields are actually very low.

Henry Hansmann, a Yale law professor who is an expert on the law and economics of nonprofit institutions, has a blunt assessment of endowments. Hansmann's contention is that all the hoarding diverts universities from their core mission of educating students and making breakthroughs in science and other fields. "They can contribute more to society by building a great university than they can by building a great endowment," he said. "A stranger from Mars who looks at private universities would probably say they are institutions whose business is to manage large pools of investments and that they run educational institutions on the side . . . to act as buffers for the investment pools."

In an article examining New York University's decision to spend current funds rather than build its endowment, Hansmann and his allies agree that administrators in other universities are wrongly making a fetish of the size of their endowments. "Saving is worthwhile only if you have a better use for the money in the future than you do now. With universities, there is no particular reason to believe that there will be a better use in the future and every reason to believe the reverse is true."

Hansmann's way of thinking has won some converts. "There is a bit of push back," said Trish Jackson, a vice president of the Council for Advancement and Support of Education. She notes, "How can we justify endowments over $1 billion? Are we shortchanging today's students for tomorrow's students?"[14]

How do we figure the cost of an endowment versus the benefits to us?

"Nonprofit organizations are not required by law to disclose information about their endowments—and many prefer not to tell the public much about the size or operations of the funds," says Harvey Lipman, writing in the *Chronicle of Philanthropy*.[15] For this reason, it is not surprising that exact figures for returns on investment or spending policies of endowments cannot be definitively stated.

The following quick formula helps to assess the amount of funds available each year to fulfill the mission of the institution. This formula attempts to pull together some of the information that is known about endowment investment and spending policies and to make some guesses that help to demonstrate the relationship between the costs and the benefits of these investments.

Using $100,000 as a basis, apply the following assumptions:

Goal of the endowment campaign	$100,000
Estimated cost of campaign (26 cents per dollar)	$26,000
Annual yield (5 percent)	$5,000
Annual amount returned to principal (2.5 percent)	($2,500)
Deduction for inflation in the nonprofit sector (1 percent)	($1,000)
Balance of annual spendable income from the fund	$1,500

To recapture the sum spent to raise the endowment, in this case $26,000, the institution will not receive a penny of appreciation for seventeen years. That is unless there is a significant change in the level of yields, the average rate of inflation, or the higher level of inflation experienced within the nonprofit sector. In some cases, endowments are reported as having much higher annual returns and in others lower returns. If you are thinking about an endowment, plug in your organization's numbers and take this formula out for a test drive.

Regarding costs, as we said in Chapter Six, the Association for Healthcare Philanthropy has studied the cost of fundraising campaigns for years. The resulting figures indicate that association members spend a median of 26 cents to raise $1. The range reported by the survey is from a cost of 56 cents to raise $1 to 12 cents for the most efficient institution. The major difference between institutions is time. Development efforts that have been in existence for between five and ten years were typically closer to 26 cents.

Retained funds invested 60 percent in stocks, 30 percent in government securities, and 10 percent in cash equivalents are considered prudent. For our purposes here we use a 5 percent return. Management fees and investment charges can total half of 1 percent annually. Recent studies challenge the notion that stocks have historically returned 10 percent, suggesting that the rate of return for stocks in the United States is closer to 5 percent.[16]

To sustain the buying power of the fund, an amount equal to an estimated five-year rolling average of inflation needs to be returned to the fund. The current estimate for inflation is 2.5 percent.

Inflation in the nonprofit world is generally considered slightly higher than in the rest of the economy. As Baumol and Bowen note in their classic study of the economics of the performing arts, inflation in the nonprofit sector is one to two full percentage points higher than in the commercial economy.[17]

We don't spend that much to raise a dollar, do we?

Clearly, one of the key assumptions included in this formula is the cost of raising a dollar—and the actual cost of raising a dollar may vary. It is often difficult to make a judgment about this because of the intense pressure in the philanthropic community to report low costs for development efforts. Institutions either underreport their costs, bury them in other accounting categories, or face losing support from donors.

If you pencil in the actual costs of raising money, you will see one reason that endowments are an inefficient fiscal device. If the total cost of raising endowments or cash reserves is included, it may well take years before institutions realize a penny of positive appreciation.

In other words, the history of endowments in this nation shows a poor track record of meeting the needs they are supposed to address. The spending policy of most trusts simply maintains the status quo for their institutions.

A wealthy donor has offered us a challenge. He will give us a million bucks to establish an endowment if we match every one of his dollars with three that we raise in the community. Shouldn't we jump at the offer?

You might want to look before you leap. Calculate the cost of raising the three-to-one match, particularly on top of your normal operating expenses, then take a hard look at the spending policy you will need to adopt to sustain the buying power of the funds, and finally figure out how long it will take before you see a penny of appreciation once you have recaptured your original investment.

Then, before accepting the donor's idea of what is good for you, ask yourself whether the donor needs to examine those numbers with you to see the consequences of the request. Lay out the relatively high cost of raising funds, the relatively low return available from endowments, and the long-term inflexibility of irrevocable trusts as instruments to prevent financial disasters.

In our experience, when confronted with the facts, donors will often reconsider the idea and offer you a much better deal. For example, the donor may decide to donate the money to be used for operations, with the understanding that you will match it three to one for the same purpose.

How can we convince donors to support us if we don't have an endowment?

Some people believe that an endowment is a feather in their cap, a symbol of a prudent and well-run organization that can afford to place surplus funds aside for later use. Others take exception to this view and see endowments as inefficient and potentially harmful to institutions in the face of an uncertain future.

While it may be true that many board and staff members want an endowment, a cash reserve, a new building, or a renovation, the competition for capital gifts, including endowment funds, is starting to have a profound and negative impact on the nonprofit sector. A study of capital giving to San Francisco nonprofits from 1988 to 1992, commissioned by the Walter and Elise Haas Fund, pointed out that the demand for capital giving created by competing campaigns would soon outstrip the supply of funds.[18]

If endowments aren't such a great deal, why does everyone else have or want one?

An endowment is a bit like chocolate cake: wonderful to dream of and delicious to eat, but not always good for you. Just because almost everyone likes chocolate, that doesn't eliminate the side effects of eating too much chocolate.

Creating, developing, and sustaining endowments entails a number of negative consequences. Endowments are costly to raise on an ongoing basis, require substantial care and feeding, and produce relatively tiny amounts of spendable income, even after your investment has been recaptured. Another way to look at endowments is that you need to raise $20 to get $1 to spend each year.

Endowments take 95 percent of the money that could be used for fulfilling your mission and place it in investments that are forever outside your reach. In addition, since the pools of resources they are drawn from are relatively inelastic, they deprive others of needed resources. They do not satisfy your needs for operational funds. They can result in diminution of services. Clients and constituents may suffer.

Still, won't it be nice to have a large endowment so we won't have to raise funds each year?

Since the operational needs of the organization continue year after year, and since endowments contribute, relatively speaking, very little to most institutions' operational budgets, the need to raise funds is not diminished by endowments. Although many donors are asked to contribute on the promise that this is a once-in-a-lifetime gift or a one-time special effort, the reality for most institutions is that they will be back at the door the next year, still needing operational funds to fulfill their mission.

Having a rainy-day fund is very desirable, isn't it? And, after all, why would we want to pay all that interest to banks?

Cash reserves or rainy-day funds always seem like a wonderful idea. The thought of having a little extra cash tucked away for a cold and blustery budgetary lapse seems so cozy and warm. And, frankly, it is nice to have some cushion in reserve. But does it make sense to have cash lying around that is expensive to raise and will produce very low rates of return given its liquidity? Credit serves exactly the same function for a nonprofit organization, and it allows you to place your hard-earned dollars into service of your mission whenever you have a need. Borrowed dollars are current, and they are inexpensive to mobilize. If you have a creditholders group in place to secure your line of credit, consider letting your banker be your rainy-day funder, and use the other capital more efficiently.

Still unconvinced about cash reserves? A cash flow analysis like the one in Exhibit 10.1 makes it clear that setting up a fully secured line of credit costs only about 11 percent as much as establishing a cash reserve.

What does the cash flow cost comparison chart indicate?

This cash flow analysis uses all three of the principles cited earlier:

- Money costs money.

- Inflation is a significant consideration.

- Time and timing are critically important in nonprofit financial management.

The application of these principles, along with some assumptions about earnings and interest, provides valuable insight on the

Exhibit 10.1. Cost Comparison of a $30,000 Cash Reserve and a $30,000 Line of Credit.

	Jan.	Feb.	Mar.	Apr.	May	June	July	Aug.	Sept.	Oct.	Nov.	Dec.	Total
INCOME	30	32	38	45	50	40	30	25	20	35	40	45	430
EXPENSE	41	40	35	32	30	35	40	45	42	35	30	25	430
RUNNING TOTAL	(11)	(19)	(16)	(3)	17	22	12	(8)	(30)	(30)	(20)	0	0
Cash reserve*													
Interest earned	67	38	49	95	166	184	146	77	0	0	35	106	963
Interest paid													
Line of credit**													
Interest earned	0	0	0	0	66	77	42	0	0	0	0	0	185
Interest paid	59	102	86	16	0	0	0	43	162	162	108	0	738
Net interest paid													553

Note: All budget figures in thousands; all interest paid and interest earned figures in dollars, rounded to the nearest whole dollar to make the chart easier to read. Surplus funds each month are invested at 4.25 percent or .00354 percent per month.

* Cash reserve = $30,000 invested at 4.25 percent or .00354 percent per month. The cash reserve was raised the prior year at a cost of $0.25 per dollar = $7,500.

** A fee for the line of credit costs .5 percent or $150 per year. Line of credit is fully secured by creditholders and carries an interest rate of 6.5 percent per year.

question of which is more cost-effective, a cash reserve or a line of credit.

In calculating the cost of this cash reserve, we used the figure of 25 cents to raise $1. Obviously this assumption can be adjusted in specific cases. On this basis it cost $7,500 to raise the reserve. During the year the cash reserve earned $963 in interest. In contrast, the line of credit carries an annual fee of .05 percent or $150 per year. Interest costs for the use of credit equals $738 and interest earned from surpluses equals $185 for a net cost of $553.

The cash reserve costs almost eleven times more than the line of credit by the end of the year. The math on this for the cost of the cash reserve is ($7,500 – $963 = $6,537) versus the cost for the line of credit, which is ($150 + $553 = $703). To assess the difference in percentage terms we divide $703 by $6,537 to come up with .1075, or about 11 percent.

Nonprofit inflation erodes the value of the cash reserve. For this example, we have assumed that inflation is 4 percent in the national economy, and two full points higher in the nonprofit sphere. This means that inflation erodes the value of the cash reserve by 6 percent per year. An amount equal to this must be placed back into the cash reserve to preserve the buying power or net value of the fund. If this is not done, the cash reserve becomes a sinking fund and will have lost one half its current value in fifteen years. That puts the ongoing cost of a $30,000 cash reserve at $1,800 per year plus the $450 required to raise that amount—less than the initial investment, but substantially more than the ongoing cost of the line of credit.

Are there any additional benefits to having a line of credit?

One final point about the advantages of using your line of credit in place of a cash reserve. When dealing with vendors, the notion of withholding payment of bills makes little sense in the nonprofit sector. Goodwill is much more important for most nonprofits. They lack the economic muscle to stiff vendors and still keep them coming back for more. The loss of discounts and the assessment of penalties for late payment are rarely worth the advantages of withholding payment.

It's true that you could use your cash reserve to pay vendors, but having funds that liquid is going to mean that you have very little interest income. Organizations that create a creditholders group and establish a secured line of credit will find that they can pay on time, reduce or eliminate penalties, gain valuable discounts, and secure far better terms with vendors. Some organizations that use a secured line of credit to pay quickly even ask their vendors to consider writing a contribution check instead of a discount. Since the vendor that you pay promptly, on delivery, loves you more than your dog does, some vendors are willing to make out tax-deductible contribution checks for up to 5 percent of the bill.

Our goal is not to deprive you of the pleasure of hanging on to surpluses or the thrill of imagining what you will do with a surprise gift. Rather, it is simply our desire to make sure that you fulfill your institution's mission for the least amount of money. In the same spirit, the next chapter turns to some questions about the value of nonprofit institutions' owning property and equipment.

11

Pros and Cons of Ownership
by a Nonprofit

Owning versus leasing has been a perennial issue in the non-profit sector for decades. This chapter offers you some choices and some reasons to consider which option is best for you when it comes time to pay for equipment and space. We dwell briefly on the issue of ownership as control, noting the economic benefits of ownership versus leasing. Then we discuss capital campaigns, along with tax-exempt borrowing and good old-fashioned leases, gifts of buildings and land, and finally what to do if you already have a building.

In keeping with our goal to make financial matters, even very complex ones, simpler and easier for you, we have developed a piece of software called the *Cash Flow Forecaster*—available as a download from the Wiley Web catalog (ordering information can be found at www.josseybass.com/go/cashflowsolution). The software incorporates the cash flow principles that we have been discussing throughout this book. The relative cost of money, the role of inflation, and issues of time and timing all play an important part in this analysis. This means that the questions built into the Real Estate Calculator all operate in a cash flow context as you explore capital campaigns, ownership, sale and lease arrangements, and different types of financing.

We are advocates for nonprofits' leasing real estate and equipment. While not categorically opposed to ownership, we remain convinced that for most nonprofits leasing often provides the best opportunity. Our experience with cash flow thinking tells us that in the long run ownership tends to be less advantageous than other arrangements that provide practical control over real estate and equipment. And if nonprofit institutions in the future will be called upon to be leaner and more financially efficient, then savings in all areas will be required.

Rather than just making a case for leasing, admittedly hard to do with board and staff members who are powerfully motivated to have their institution own its facilities and equipment, it makes good sense to look at various points of view with a cash flow lens and let you decide for yourself.

Any comparison of the cost and benefits of real estate in the nonprofit sector is dictated by three considerations:

- The hard issues that establish the actual financial costs and benefits of any option

- The special circumstances that apply to a specific institution, which may make one choice more attractive than another

- The soft issues that represent the values and wishes of the members of the board and staff

With so many different issues at play, it is no wonder that real estate questions in the nonprofit sector are complex. However, that does not make it impossible to identify the issues from a cash flow perspective and compare and contrast them.

Isn't it every American's dream to own?

Owning property has a lot of emotional appeal to folks just trying to get their mission accomplished. It feels safe and secure to own your facilities and equipment. For some, it is like a merit badge, a sign that you have finally arrived. The new building is a landmark, a signal that you are in the big time. So talking about real estate evokes powerful feelings.

The soft issues of value and preference often get confused with the hard, strictly monetary issues. While a building is a tangible asset, its financial value can be realized only when it is sold. Then the proceeds are not distributed as they would be in a business. Instead, they are typically used for funding program expenses, or for acquiring a new facility. In the meantime, because nonprofits often do not pay taxes, depreciation is essentially meaningless; it has no tax benefits for tax-exempt organizations.

All right, we know that our accountant is not going to let us get away with defaming depreciation, but truthfully, how many non-profit organizations are prepared to establish plant funds to com-pensate for the real declining value of a building? (*Plant funds* are reserves designed to provide money for replacement and renova-tions of facilities.) Few nonprofits can afford to sustain large liquid plant funds, and even if they could, the costs of renovation are not deductible.

Under the headline "For Nonprofits, Owning Is Becoming the Wave of the Past," the *New York Times* recently noted that a growing number of nonprofit organizations have been selling their buildings in New York, partly because real estate sales in the city are strong and can provide funds for critical missions, but also because many non-profit organizations realize that leasing space can be much easier and less expensive than keeping a property in good condition.[19]

How can we control our space if we do not own it?

Many nonprofits believe that real estate ownership is a means of con-trolling their destiny. The story goes something like this: *Control is important. If we own our building, we have control.* This is a com-mon assertion in nonprofit boardrooms across the nation. Yet own-ership and control are not necessarily the same thing. For example, owning property that you can't afford to maintain can have disastrous effects on your program budget if the roof starts to leak, or the foundation shifts.

A nonprofit that owns a building it cannot afford to operate, or cannot maintain in excellent condition, is in deep trouble. Serving two masters—social purpose and fiscal solvency—makes it difficult to allocate resources to a plant fund when the orphans are hungry.

Control, on the other hand, can be secured through well-crafted long-term leases that bind the parties to a set of understandings that are workable and fair. By spelling out terms and conditions in advance, a nonprofit organization can plan for its future expenditures without worrying about unanticipated disasters.

Although some believe that contracts are made to be broken, we still have faith that a well-crafted long-term lease, with an option to renew, can go a long way to ensure that the nonprofit organization is protected, along with the property owner.

What about our particular circumstance?

Let's talk about some of the issues that define the circumstances faced by a specific institution. For example, if an institution wishes to acquire a building, and it has access to wealthy donors willing to contribute enough funds to purchase or construct the facility, it might explore the feasibility of conducting a capital campaign. If the campaign has a high probability of success and if the costs both in time and effort can be endured up front, this approach is likely to be the least expensive choice. After all, if someone else will pay for a facility, and if the only expenses are meeting the annual operating costs, plus a little extra for a plant fund, this is going to be cheaper than renting or acquiring a conventional mortgage.

Notice the whole series of conditions that can have a profound effect on the choice—access to wealthy donors being the most obvious. The ability to conduct a campaign that is cost-effective is another. Cost-effectiveness is influenced by factors that may be beyond the control of the institution, such as the number of capital campaigns simultaneously under way within a community, or the state of the economy, particularly as it affects wealthy donors. Moreover, there is the issue of time that the campaign will require, along with the time that construction takes, if that is the option at hand.

Okay, what about the costs of a capital campaign?

Everyone wants a capital campaign. After all, having others pay for your facility, while still maintaining the tax advantages of being a nonprofit, can seem pretty compelling. Not only that, the process has been fine-tuned over the years by handsomely tailored consultants in graciously appointed firms across the nation.

Still, conducting a capital campaign has some real risks, and even though campaigns that stall or fail generally get little publicity, it happens. News about capital campaigns that fail to reach their goal is just the type of information that nonprofit organizations conceal in their public statements, for obvious reasons.

A study of capital giving to San Francisco nonprofits from 1988 to 1992, commissioned by the Walter and Elise Haas Fund, points out that the demand for capital giving can soon outstrip the supply.[20]

The study reached five main conclusions:

- Capital giving is growing significantly faster than overall giving.

- The aspirations of San Francisco nonprofit organizations for capital donations would appear to outstrip future donors' giving capacity.

- Many campaigns are likely to fail or fall significantly below their targets; alternatively, if they succeed, there will be a significant shift in charitable giving that may negatively affect many organizations.

- Foundations played a major role in the growth of capital giving. This increase was made possible by unusual growth in assets in the period under study.

- Capital campaigns have the effect of redistributing total charitable giving, reducing income to some recipients and increasing income to others.

What this study highlights is the problem many nonprofit institutions face when considering a capital campaign. The goal of getting the money up front from a capital campaign may prove to be elusive in the face of intense competition from other campaigns. You run the risk that your efforts will be less than successful—in which case, it may not be possible to raise all the funds needed to actually construct, buy, or renovate the facilities.

This is also a very costly process in terms of time. Capital campaigns can take three to five years in some cases, and while all this is going on, dollars for operations still need to be raised year after year. Cash flow analysis demonstrates how important it is to keep a sharp eye on operational expenses during any fundraising effort, and particularly capital campaigns.

Institutions contemplating a capital campaign need to pay careful attention to the cost of raising money. Successful capital campaigns must include some additional funding to account for donor fatigue after the goal is achieved. Often campaigns also include an endowment to provide operating funds in the future. Mobilizing all that money up front can be very expensive and time-consuming.

Perhaps we should get a conventional mortgage? What about other choices?

Any institution planning to enter into a conventional mortgage will be keenly interested in the current cost of money. The amount of interest to be paid over the life of the loan can be a substantial concern, even if interest rates are not too high. Unable to trade off any of the finance costs through a tax deduction, the nonprofit with a conventional mortgage will pay for the building, the financing, and the expenses associated with facility maintenance.

Hey, we are tax exempt, why not pursue a tax-exempt bond for our facilities?

Just saying *tax-exempt financing* resonates sweetly in the minds of many leaders of nonprofit institutions. The reason why tax-exempt financing often pencils out better than other choices is that the money is cheaper. And, as you remember, the cost of money is an essential consideration in cash flow thinking.

If you compare two mortgages, one with tax-exempt financing and one without, it does not require a genius to figure out which is the better deal. But, here again, the circumstance of the institution plays a part. The nonprofit that has a strong financial track record and good credit is going to be much more attractive to the folks who package the bonds that ultimately underwrite the mortgage. So as the nonprofit institution proceeds with its exploration of tax-exempt financing, its own fiscal position may be a key factor in determining if the financial arrangement is possible.

Whatever happened to plain, old-fashioned leases?

So far, we have looked at choices that involve ownership, through a capital campaign, through a conventional mortgage, or a non-conventional (read tax-exempt) mortgage.

In a traditional lease, the cost of financing the deal is also a factor that may ultimately influence the cost to the nonprofit institution. While it is true that rentals are a function of what the local market will bear and therefore not just a matter of the landlord adding up all the costs to establish the price, the cost of money is still a major consideration. If the financing costs more because interest rates are higher, then it will likely have some impact on the cost of the lease.

Another circumstance is the availability of space in the local real estate market. When vacancies are common, leases tend to be cheaper. If space is tight, costs go up. Availability coupled with interest rates are factors beyond the institution's control.

Still, leasing has its charms. It is incremental, in the sense that you only have to raise and pay the rent once a month, and that can provide more money for your mission. Leasing also shifts the costs of ongoing maintenance to the landlord, which in some cases is a blessing.

Leasing means living light, not owning the facility with all its attendant headaches. For many nonprofit institutions, the flexibility of leasing means that when it's time to move on, say because you have outgrown the space, you can fulfill the terms of your lease and move on.

What about the nonconventional lease?

In this case, a socially motivated person or a group of socially motivated people offers a nonprofit a lower rate than the market might bear, while still deriving some of the benefits that come from owning real estate. The depreciation, the interest on financing, and the cost of operations and maintenance expenses all have a tax consequence for the owner that can sweeten the deal.[21]

A foundation, an institutional endowment, or even a donor-directed financial service organization might be persuaded to enhance the credit of a nonprofit institution by providing a *deficiency guarantee*. This terrible-sounding term is actually a very good thing. It means acquiring a form of insurance for the credit, whereby (sometimes for a fee) an unrelated party agrees to cover the cost of the rent in the event that the nonprofit is unable to do so. In those instances, in which this type of insurance is in play, the socially motivated building owner has a reduced risk that can translate into cheaper financing, and may be able to offer the nonprofit a much better deal.

In this kind of unconventional lease, the feasibility involves two factors. One is the willingness of a socially motivated—in contrast to a purely profit motivated—landlord to offer the nonprofit institution a preferential deal on the real estate. The second is the insurance provided by foundations, endowments, or by donor-directed financial service firms. With one or both of these opportunities, the nonconventional lease can be of great benefit to the nonprofit institution and not a bad deal either for the landlord or the financial players providing the insurance.

We own our building and are not interested in a capital campaign. What choices do we have?

From a cash flow perspective, a sale and leaseback arrangement might work well for you. In this case, if the deal is attractive enough to potential investors, and if the time value of money is factored in, this approach puts money in the institution's pocket for the building and establishes a long-term rental relationship.

If the institution takes a portion of the funds paid to it as part of the sale and prepays its rental for a number of years, it can take advantage of the money's loss of value over time (net present value). In other words, a smart landlord and an equally smart nonprofit tenant might both benefit from the prepayment of rent since both understand that a dollar today is worth more than the same dollar next year.

The circumstances that make sale and leaseback favorable include having a building of sufficient value to attract investors willing to engage in this type of transaction, or having a credit history strong enough to justify the investors' purchasing or building a building to suit the institution. In all cases, the sale and leaseback option results in structuring a long-term lease.

So pitting the capital campaign against the sale and leaseback arrangement requires that specific circumstances be in play to allow the choice to be useful. It is easy to declare a capital campaign. It may be much more difficult to conduct it and still sustain the annual fundraising necessary to keep your operations running smoothly. On the other hand, the conversion of facilities into immediately available working capital can be explored with little or no cost to the institution.

What if someone wants to give us a building?

Accepting gifts always seems like a wonderful idea. After all, we all love presents. If someone wants or needs to give you a building, you can accept with gratitude, especially if you have made provision for someone else to own and operate it. Why not arrange the donation— and then turn the depreciation in the building over to a business- person who can use it? Because you wish to control the space, find a businessperson who will accept the value of the building as partial prepaid rent and utilities for a period of time. You get to control the space on a long-term lease, the donor gets to use the value of the building as a tax deduction, and the businessperson gets the oppor- tunity to enjoy the tax benefits of ownership.

What about someone wanting to give us land to hold until the next Ice Age?

Gifts of land are another category entirely. Often the donor will request that the land be maintained in perpetuity, with or without financial provision for its stewardship. So the tiny nonprofit Land Trust, which struggles to get a five-person quorum at its monthly meetings, is granted a couple of hundred acres of pristine wildlife refugee along with the responsibility to maintain it as a public ben- efit forever. In this case, the group typically has no option to sell the land or to develop it. This type of transaction requires plenty of forethought on the part of the recipient and some serious plans for how the future financial responsibility associated with this land will be managed.[22]

We already have a building. Why wouldn't we want to keep it?

You can. But you might want to consider—just consider, mind you—the possibility that your institution might be better off if you sold the building to an interested party, secured a substantial long-term lease that gave you lots of control, and used a significant portion of the proceeds from the sale to fund your rental for many, many years. Then, when the roof fails in the next snowstorm, someone else's insurance can cover the costs, and someone else—who can derive tax benefits unavailable to you—can take care of the consequences. While all this is happening, you can continue providing a public good.

Isn't it true that our building gives us equity for the future?

If your nonprofit were a business and had equity to offer, then the building would serve that purpose. But because your organization is a nonprofit, all the building has is a paper asset value until it is sold. And again, the proceeds will either go to a program (yours, or someone else's if you've hit a wall and need to liquidate the organization) or a new facility. Why not let the future be now?

Shouldn't we consider real estate as an investment opportunity?

Ownership is often justified by assuming that property can be acquired and held as an investment that will yield future profits. Nonprofit organizations are meant to provide social benefits through their mission, not to compete as tax-exempt real estate holding companies. For this reason, social purposes should have first claim on all donated funds. Buildings do not lower program costs, and the funds used to acquire buildings are no longer available to pursue the institution's mission.[23]

Our donors will not support operations, but they will fund buildings. What can we do?

Some nonprofits use the "edifice complex" to rationalize acquiring real estate. They claim that contributors are willing to donate for bricks and mortar, but not for less concrete purposes such as research, operating expenses, or scholarships. Cultural organizations, colleges and universities, and hospitals are especially likely to feel they have to deal with this phenomenon.

However, often the edifice complex is actually encouraged by the conventional wisdom of development officers and fundraising consultants, not the donors. When nonprofits analyze the long-term costs and benefits of owning versus leasing, the financial gains of leasing are often compelling. These numbers, presented in conjunction with the costs and the risks associated with conducting a major capital campaign, often make less concrete funding needs attractive to donors with business acumen.

Are you still urging us to lease?

We advise our nonprofit clients to try not to own things that are not disposable. Leasing is possible in many different forms, including concessionary leases (a *concessionary lease* is one that is offered at below normal market rates, usually because the landlord supports the social purpose of the organization). For this reason a concessionary lease is often less expensive than commercial rental. The reason for not owning is simply that nonprofits have no incentive to own.

Ownership offers no tax advantages for tax-exempt organizations. Depreciation takes place, but your institution funds it at the cost of fulfilling its social purpose. When things wear out or need to be replaced, it makes more sense to have people who can derive benefit from investing do so, rather than burdening the organization and the people you serve with increased costs. This does not mean that every single nonprofit organization should lease, of course. What we are suggesting is that the comparison of different options to ownership should be given a fair hearing before the court adjourns.

Is there a simple and easy way to do all this electronically?

Real estate strategies can be confusing. So (as noted at the beginning of this chapter) we developed a program we call the Real Estate Calculator, which is linked to the Cash Flow Forecaster to help you compare and contrast different scenarios in which hard issues, such as costs that can be nailed down, are examined.

The educational information provided in the software will help inform your choices by giving you a sense of some of the pros and cons associated with owning versus leasing. This information can then be matched up with your specific circumstances to guide you in making a decision in the best interest of your institution.

What the calculator cannot do is to help you assess the importance of the soft issues, those values that often tip board and staff members one way or another when confronted with real estate questions. If you believe that owning a building is more important than anything else, then there really isn't much of a contest. Regardless of the cost or long-term benefit, this value makes attempts at comparison meaningless. However, if you are willing to set aside the Great American Dream syndrome, look beyond the gut issues, and balance off the costs and benefits of ownership versus leasing, then comparison is the only way to go.

Along with the issues surrounding real estate, the questions raised about the effectiveness of nonprofit enterprises, when viewed from a cash flow perspective, are worth considering. In the next chapter we share some ideas that may challenge your basic assumptions about nonprofits and their enterprises.

12

Earned Revenue and Discounts

We live in an entrepreneurial society. So, it's not surprising that board members are likely to be champions of earning more revenue.

In this chapter we explore some of the constraints to earning revenue and offer a few cautionary notes about nonprofit earned income strategies. We demonstrate how focusing on cash flow helps highlight the importance of working capital to nonprofit organizations, and we again examine the cost of money as an operational issue.

We all love a bargain, but the question is: *At what cost?* We feature a small section on the generous though sometimes misguided tendency for some nonprofits to give away the store.

To start us off, Clara Miller's article, "The Looking-Glass World of Nonprofit Money: Managing in For-Profit's Shadow Universe," notes that at a time when both government and philanthropy are encouraging all sorts of social enterprise and earned income models in the nonprofit sector, particularly health care and education, the whole operating environment of nonprofit management needs to be better understood.[24]

Miller writes that nonprofit organizations are in a difficult position when it comes to relating their prices to the expenses they incur. In commercial ventures you close an unprofitable business, but in the nonprofit sector this lack of profit is just par for the course. Mission drives nonprofits, and as a result institutions continue to offer shelter, medical care, disaster relief, and other services to people who are unable to pay for them.

Moreover, other factors contribute to the lack of profitability. Much of the nonprofit field is labor intensive or requires highly skilled practitioners. It also suffers from economies of scale. You can't simply ramp up the numbers in the quest for profitability. As Miller notes, "if we increase class sizes to 100, all kindergartens will be profitable."

Most board members are aware that restrictions or "strings" are often attached to grants. Fewer are aware of the restrictions surrounding earned revenue in the nonprofit sector. In many nonprofit situations, this means that a third party—government, foundation, donor, or corporate contribution committee—dictates how money will be spent on the consumers of the service. These consumers of nonprofit services are often the elderly, the homeless, parentless children, impoverished adults, and others without the means to pay the full cost of the service. In some cases, consumers may be technically able but unwilling to pay for the full cost—say, of the opera, or of their children's private school education. Third parties make up the difference in much of the nonprofit world.

Prices to consumers are often inelastic, regardless of who pays. Just how much more can children or low-income people be expected to pay? The consequence is that as more service is provided the financial position of nonprofits can be seriously compromised. It is the moral imperative rather than any expectation of profit that keeps nonprofit staff on the job.

Miller makes the key point that price inelasticity represents double jeopardy for management. The problem is that there is a lack of profit-generated working capital to fund growth and a continuing need for larger subsidies as growth takes place.

What is working capital?

Working capital, according to the second edition of the *Random House Dictionary of the English Language*, is the amount of capital needed to carry on a business. Accountants use the term to refer to current assets minus current liabilities. A third definition is liquid assets, as distinguished from fixed capital assets. We think of working capital as the money that nonprofits need to conduct their operations.

In another book that we have written for Jossey-Bass, we make the case that it is lack of access to working capital that poses the greatest obstacle to success in the nonprofit sector. Since individual and institutional donors, foundations, and government agencies continue to resist paying their full share for the operational costs of nonprofit institutions, we urge our clients to take matters into their own hands. By adopting our cash flow approach to budgeting, forecasting, and monitoring, by forming a creditholders group, and then by heading to the bank these organizations can obtain working capital without having to accumulate vast reserves. In combination with revenues that are raised and earned, the borrowed dollars can be used at times when they are most needed.

Why isn't our auction the answer?

To make up for the lack of access to working capital nonprofits tend to develop subsidy businesses. In other words, losses in the mission-driven component of nonprofits stimulate the creation of "secondary businesses" to make up the difference in unrestricted funds. So bake sales, special events, parking lots, gift shops, bookstores, and bingo are scattered across the nonprofit landscape. Of course, there are costs associated with the auction or even the car wash, and these only add to the complexity of the administration of nonprofits. Yet such secondary activities are so completely integrated into organizational thinking about earned revenue that many board members focus their attention almost exclusively on mini-enterprises like these.

As we noted earlier, it costs money to raise money and to earn money. The vast majority of large businesses in American society operate with a relatively small margin of profit. Margins of 5 percent, 6 percent, or 7 percent are not uncommon in the ranks of competitive corporations. Do nonprofits, already strapped for cash, have the money to invest in running a store that will bring in a surplus of less than 10 percent? Many do not, and those that do often fail to grasp how time-consuming and demanding successful business undertakings can be. Will the time and effort devoted to obtaining revenue be a drain on the organization and the social purpose for which the organization was chartered? In other words, when does the quest for income overwhelm the mission of the institution?

In boardrooms across the country, earned revenue strategies are hatched and fueled by the idea that nonprofits can be more efficient than businesses. The role of volunteers is often cited in these discussions. Volunteers admittedly reduce some costs, but they also add costs through turnover and their need for flexible scheduling and efficient coordination. In the short run, volunteerism may be great, but in an entrepreneurial environment, in the long run it is not necessarily more effective than a paid workforce.

Isn't offering discount sales to season ticket holders a good way to make money?

Subscription campaigns have a short and checkered history. They were conceived as a way to fill seats and the organization's coffers to cover seasonal deficits and to front the costs for new productions. Instead, they have proven to be costly and, in many ways, questionable as a financial strategy.

Here's why, from a cash flow perspective. When an organization offers a discount of, say, 15 percent to subscribers, it is taxing itself at a higher rate of interest than a bank might charge to lend. Added to the discount are the costs of the subscription campaign, which can be as much as 5 percent of the annual budget. In addition, having two campaigns, one for fundraising and the other for subscriptions, frequently confuses both donors and subscribers.

One evening, we got a call at dinner from a local theater asking us to subscribe, offering a 15 percent discount to do so. I assumed that this campaign probably cost at least 5 percent to conduct, so the net cost to the theater was 20 percent. Less than an hour later, we got a call from another telemarketing firm, working for the same theater, telling us how much our donation was needed to cover costs. We did a little math on the phone, and, sure enough, the difference was close to 20 percent. I suggested that the theater not offer financial discounts, but the person on the other end of the phone wanted a pledge, not free advice.

The next day, I called the manager of the theater and made an appointment to discuss this interesting paradox. During our meeting, I asked how the theater's board and staff had arrived at a 15 percent discount. He said the number had sounded like it would be a good inducement to prospective subscribers.

At that point in the discussion, I explained that I had, some years earlier, conducted an informal survey of subscribers in a city-wide assessment of subscription campaigns. My results suggested that few subscribers were greatly influenced by the discounting of their ticket price. In fact, the vast majority told me that they subscribed because they supported their cultural institutions as a general policy. Oh, they would be happy to get preferential seating or greater flexibility in ticket exchanges, but most would be just as happy to get a nonfinancial perk such as a cup of good coffee and a cookie at intermission or an invitation to a special event. I suggested that the theater check with its own subscribers to confirm or refute my statements. I pointed out that my research indicated that the people who are most price sensitive are the single-ticket purchasers. Yet most theaters charge them the highest prices and offer them the fewest benefits.

"Drop the financial discounts," I said, "and serve them fresh-roasted coffee and cookies instead." The theater manager eyed me coldly and said, "Just how do you propose that I find the money I need to pay off last year's deficit and to pay for this year's productions?" I answered, "Look, form a creditholders group who will support your mission; then go to the bank and engage in a little fully secured borrowing. See if your budget and balance sheet don't look better in a year. Get your money at or below prime, rather than paying the equivalent of 20 percent in interest through all those discounts and campaign costs."

Together we did the math, and the figures were impressive. The theater manager said he would try it, and as I was leaving I suggested that he drop day-of-performance single-ticket prices for a while to bring in new audience members and see if attendance increased. A year later, the theater was functioning much better, having effected each of these changes—and we got only one call soliciting funds for its operations. Still in the middle of supper, of course.

Because of the tremendous curiosity about earned revenue in the nonprofit field, literature has developed that provides encouragement and some helpful tips. Much of this activity seems to us to be evoked by a desire on the part of nonprofit institutions and their supporters to find a self-determined method to mobilize working capital. This makes complete sense when the funding environment is as turbulent as it has been in recent years.

Perhaps the question needs to be asked in a different way. For example, we know that nonprofit organizations are allowed to raise funds through gifts and grants. We also know that despite IRS regulations on "unrelated business income," many nonprofit organizations must have earned revenue to survive. How would most colleges fare without tuition or hospitals without payments from patients or their insurers? So there is no question that nonprofits need money. The question, it seems to us, is what type of money they most need.

Our response is that working capital is the most vitally important type of money that nonprofit organizations require. Of course, project-specific grants throw off some money for administration and overhead, and similarly earnings from fees for service are important, but the dollar that is needed for day-to-day operations still must be there for the institution to function.

What other ways can we use to obtain access to working capital?

Cash flow budgeting, forecasting, and monitoring open the door to the use of credit; when combined with the other two types of money, they create the financial base necessary for the healthy functioning of nonprofit institutions. For this reason, we encourage board and staff members to think of funds in the broadest possible sense, including the use of credit to borrow when needed. In other words, we are asking you to think about money in a different way.

Final Thoughts

Cash flow has been the focus of our attention. We have compared conventional budgets with cash flow budgets. We have championed the use of footnotes to make sure everyone on the board understands the numbers. We have shown you how the Cash Flow Forecaster can be used to convert cash flow budgets into forecasts and easily understood monitoring reports that can be quickly generated.

Along the way we have introduced the concepts of creditholders, collateral, and the importance of working capital for nonprofit institutions. With a tip of our hat to bankers and a couple of knocks on endowments and cash reserves, we have urged you to think about keeping your organization as lean and as financially efficient as possible.

Before sending you on your way, we could not resist one last round of recommendations. Please give these thoughts a moment to swirl around in your mind before launching yourself into the business at hand—guiding your nonprofit institution toward success.

A Summary of Recommendations

Budgeting

- Create a cash flow budget on a month-by-month basis.
- Use footnotes to explain every item on your budget.
- Use a three-line summary budget for reporting at board meetings, with backup available for interested parties.

Monitoring

- Prepare cash flow reports that demonstrate the progress you are making on a month-by-month basis.

Forecasting

- Think about the future in terms of strategy.
- Quickly generate different scenarios to create a rolling forecast.

Line of credit

- Establish a creditholders group.
- Obtain a line of credit from your bank.

Use of capital

- Remember that deficits in nonprofits are not like losses in business; address them with term credit.
- Rather than creating or maintaining a cash reserve, endowment, or quasi-endowment, use your capacity to borrow inexpensively to meet your cash flow requirements.

Vendors

- Pay your vendors quickly. Let them know you will pay quickly in the future.

- Ask your vendors to offer you a discount for quick payment, but not off the bill. Instead, have them write a check for a tax-deductible contribution to your organization.

- Generate and sustain good will with your vendors and your community using your line of credit.

Leasing

- Lease buildings and equipment. Consider owning nothing, if possible, that is not disposable.

Earned revenue

- Carefully monitor the costs of subsidiary businesses in relation to the income they produce.

- Offer nonfinancial rewards rather than discounts to attract customers or audience members.

Notes

1. *It's Simple! Money Matters for the Nonprofit Board Member* (1999) was awarded the Alliance for Nonprofit Management 2000 Terry McAdam Award, Honorable Mention, for outstanding contribution to the advancement of the nonprofit sector.

2. J. G. Siegel and J. K. Shim, *Accounting Handbook*, 2nd ed. (Hauppauge, N.Y.: Barron's, 1995).

3. J. A. Paulos, *A Mathematician Plays the Stock Market* (New York: Basic Books, 2003), p. 115.

4. Yogi Berra in a television commercial, complete with quacking duck.

5. Y. Zhao, "As College Endowments Slip, Tuition Increases Fill the Void," NYTimes.com, Feb. 22, 2002.

6. B. Marten, "University Reports Deficit," Stanford Daily Online Edition, Feb. 6, 2003.

7. J. Hope and R. Fraser, *Beyond Budgeting: How Managers Can Break Free from the Annual Performance Trap* (Boston: Harvard Business School Press, 2003).

8. J. Zweig, "Peter's Uncertainty Principle," *Money Magazine*, Nov. 2004, p. 144. For those who have not read Peter Bernstein's *Against the Gods: The Remarkable Story of Risk* (New York: Wiley, 1996), make a point of adding it to your list to understand the critical relationship between gambling and investing, all made possible by the development of probability theory.

9. Association for Health Care Philanthropy, "Annual Report on Giving, 2003," part of an annual survey conducted of association membership.

10. J. Surowiecki, "The Financial Page: What Ails Us," *New Yorker*, July 7, 2003, p. 27. "Baumol's cost disease" (see Note 16) is a term used by economists to refer to a condition in institutions where productivity is flat and costs and prices keep going up. William Baumol, an NYU economist, is credited with the diagnosis of this phenomenon in the 1960s. A recent study by economists Jack Triplett and Barry Bosworth demonstrates that among the service businesses that have been least productive in recent years you'll find education, insurance, health care, and entertainment.

11. T. A. McLaughlin, *Streetsmart Financial Basics for Nonprofit Managers* (New York: Wiley, 1995).

12. R. Linzer, "Creditholders," *Practical Philanthropist*, July 1992.

13. A. Meckstroth and P. Arnsberger, "A 20-Year Review of the Nonprofit Sector, 1975–1995," *Statistics of Income (SOI) Bulletin*, Fall 1998.

14. K. R. Weiss, "NYU Earns Respect," *Los Angeles Times*, March 22, 2000. (Weiss is the *Times* education writer; this article includes both Henry Hansmann's comments and that of Trish Jackson.)

15. H. Lipman, "Measuring Endowments: How the Survey Was Conducted," *Chronicle of Philanthropy: The Chronicle of Education*, Special Edition on Endowments, May 27–28, 2004, p. B2.

16. D. Futrelle, "Build Wealth in Any Market," *Money Magazine*, Sept. 2004, p. 84. The article discusses James Garland's research for Ibbotson Associates, a financial research consulting firm, which appeared in the *Journal of Investing*.

   Another skeptical view of the risks and rewards associated with investment is provided by the mathematician Benoit Mandelbrot in B. Mandelbrot, *The (Mis) Behavior of Markets: A Fractal View of Risk, Ruin, and Reward* (New York: Basic Books, 2004).

17. W. J. Baumol and W. Bowen, *Performing Arts: The Economic Dilemma* (Cambridge, Mass.: MIT Press, 1966).

18. M. Blake, "A Study of Capital Giving to San Francisco Nonprofits, 1988–1992" (San Francisco: Walter & Elise Haas Fund, 1994).

19. S. Siwolop, "For Nonprofits, Owing Is Becoming the Wave of the Past," NYTimes.com, March 30, 2005.

20. Association for Health Care Philanthropy, "Annual Report on Giving, 2003."

21. R. Nessen, "Real Estate Finance and Taxation: Structuring Complex Transactions" (Boston: Robert L. Nessen of CRIC Capital, LLC, 1998).

22. C. Miller, "The Gift Horse or Trojan Horse: A Thorough Physical Is Critical," *Nonprofit Quarterly*, 2004, *11*(2). Both authors were instrumental in establishing the first Land Trust in Washington State. They have firsthand experience with the challenges associated with balancing a mission devoted to perpetual stewardship of land with the organizational capabilities of small, informal groups of volunteers.

23. J. T. Bennett and T. J. DiLorenzo, *Unhealthy Charities* (New York: Basic Books, 1994).

24. C. Miller, "The Looking-Glass World of Nonprofit Money: Managing in For-Profit's Shadow Universe," *Nonprofit Quarterly*, 2005, *12*(1).

Additional References

A number of sources contributed to the ideas reflected in this book. This list is provided for those who have a little extra time for reading and a compelling need to learn more about where we got some of our ideas about money matters.

Anthes, E., Cronin, J., and Jackson, M., *The Nonprofit Board Book*. West Memphis, Ark.: Independent Community Consultants, 1985.

Arnsberger, P. "Private Foundations and Charitable Trusts, 1995." In *Statistics of Income (SOI) Bulletin*, Winter, 1998–1999. Washington, D.C.: Statistics of Income Division, Internal Revenue Service.

Bolman, L. G., and Deal, T. E. *Reframing Organizations: Artistry, Choice, and Leadership*. San Francisco: Jossey-Bass, 1994.

Bryson, J. M. *Strategic Planning for Public and Nonprofit Organizations*. San Francisco: Jossey-Bass, 1990.

DiMaggo, P. J. *Nonprofit Enterprises in the Arts*. Oxford, England: Oxford University Press, 1986.

Dowie, M. *American Foundations: An Investigative History*. Cambridge, Mass.: MIT Press, 2001.

Futrelle, D. "Build Wealth in Any Market." *Money Magazine*, Sept. 2004.

Gardner, H. *Changing Minds: The Art and Science of Changing Our Own and Other People's Minds*. Boston: Harvard Business School Press, 2004.

Gladwell, M. *The Tipping Point: How Little Things Can Make a Big Difference*. New York: Little, Brown, 2002.

Hammack, D. C., and Young, D. R. *Nonprofit Organizations in the Market Economy*. San Francisco: Jossey-Bass, 1993.

Hansmann, H., in Brimelow, P., "Professor Scrooge: Colleges Cry Poor Mouth to Their Alumni Even While Their Endowments Soar." *Forbes*, Oct. 19, 1998, p. 60.

Hopkins, B. R. *The Legal Answer Book for Nonprofit Organizations*. New York: Wiley, 1992.

Internal Revenue Service, Statistics of Income. *Compendium of Studies of Tax-Exempt Organizations, 1974–87*. Washington, D.C.: U.S. Government Printing Office, 1991.

Internal Revenue Service, Statistics of Income. *Compendium of Studies of Tax-Exempt Organizations, 1986–1992*, Vol. 2. Washington, D.C.: U.S. Government Printing Office, 1991.

Kauffman, S. A. *Origins of Order: Self-Organization and Selection in Evolution*. Oxford, England: Oxford University Press, 1991.

Kotler, P., and Andreason, A. *Strategic Marketing for Nonprofit Organizations*. Upper Saddle River, N.J.: Prentice Hall, 1982.

Krugman, P. *The Self-Organizing Economy*. Malden, Mass.: Blackwell, 1996.

Linzer, R. "Borrowing: A Resource for Nonprofits." *Chronicle of Non-Profit Enterprise*, Jan. 1989.

Linzer, R. "Why You Want to Borrow from Banks." *Taft Nonprofit Executive*, 1989, 8(8), 4.

Linzer, R. "Endowments: The Other Side of the Coin." *Chronicle of Non-Profit Enterprise*, July 1992.

Linzer, R. "Using Credit to Stabilize Cash Flow." *Journal of the Land Trust Alliance*, 1993, Winter.

Linzer, R. "Charities Should Borrow Money, Not Hoard It." *Chronicle of Philanthropy*, July 24, 1997, Opinion Section.

Linzer R., and Linzer, A. *It's Easy! Money Matters for Nonprofit Managers*. Indianola, Wash.: Port Madison Press, 2001.

Rudney, G. "The Scope and Dimensions of Nonprofit Activity." In W. W. Powell (Ed.), *The Nonprofit Sector: A Research Handbook*. New Haven, Conn.: Yale University Press, 1987.

Salamon, L., and Abramson, A. "Managing Foundation Assets: An Analysis of Foundation Investment and Payout Procedures and Performance." Council on Foundations, 1991.

Schor, J. B. *The Overworked American: The Unexpected Decline of Leisure*. New York: Basic Books, 1992.

Skloot, E. *Smart Borrowing, A Nonprofit's Guide to Working with Banks*. New York: New York Community Trust, 1989.

Stacey, R. D. *Managing the Unknowable: Strategic Boundaries Between Order and Chaos in Organizations*. San Francisco: Jossey-Bass, 1992.

Stevens, S., and Anderson, L. *All the Way to the Bank: Smart Money Management for Tomorrow's Nonprofit*. St. Paul, Minn.: Stevens Group, 1997.

Strathern, P. *A Brief History of Economic Genius*. New York: TEXERE LLC, 2001.

Tower, J. "Ginnie Mae Pool No. 1: A Revolution Is Paid Off." *Bloomsberg News*, as reprinted in the *Seattle Times*, Sept. 19, 1999.

Waldrop, M. M. *Complexity: The Emerging Science at the Edge of Order and Chaos*. New York: Touchstone, 1992.

Weisbrod, B. *The Nonprofit Economy*. Cambridge, Mass.: Harvard University Press, 1998.

Williamson, P. J. "Spending Policy for College and University Endowments." Wilton, Conn.: Commonfund, 1979.

Index